SCOTLAND'S WINGS

SCOTLAND'S WINGS

TRIUMPH AND TRAGEDY IN THE SKIES

ROBERT JEFFREY

BLACK & WHITE PUBLISHING

First published in the UK in 2022 by
Black & White Publishing Ltd
Nautical House, 104 Commercial Street, Edinburgh EH6 6NF

A division of Bonnier Books UK
4th Floor, Victoria House, Bloomsbury Square, London, WC1B 4DA
Owned by Bonnier Books
Sveavägen 56, Stockholm, Sweden

The publisher has made every reasonable effort to contact copyright holders
of images in the picture section. Any errors are inadvertent and anyone who
for any reason has not been contacted is invited to write to the publisher so
that a full acknowledgement can be made in subsequent editions of this work.

A CIP catalogue record for this book is available from the British Library.

ISBN: 978 1 78530 406 4

1 3 5 7 9 10 8 6 4 2

Typeset by Data Connection
Printed and bound in Great Britain by Clays Ltd, Elcograf S.p.A.

www.blackandwhitepublishing.com

Scotland's Wings *is dedicated to*
Marie Jeffrey and Lise Jeffrey

CONTENTS

Introduction

Chairman Mao famously said that a journey of a thousand miles begins with the first step. For me a journey of thousands of words and countless hours of pleasurable reading and research began, not with a step, but with a searching glance up at a menacingly grey Scottish sky one day in the early 1950s. I was in the playground of King's Park Senior Secondary School in a douce middle class south Glasgow suburb. My class had been invited to put aside our jotters and leave our desks to see a remarkable sight. It was the first time this had happened in my schooling. Was it just the wise decision of our own "headie"? Or was the release ordered by a forward-thinking Education Department? It was the latter, though that was not something that concerned us as we waited excitedly for the appearance over our heads of the *Bristol Brabazon* airliner, the technological wonder of the age that filled the feature pages of magazines and newspapers for months. This was to be the future in the air.

When it appeared at last, high in the west, I remember most clearly the curious growling sound produced by the Centaurus engines that held the giant aloft. The immense power of these innovative engines drove eight propellers, for this was, of course, before the time of modern jet engines. Lots of power was a must for this gigantic and innovative aircraft which approached the size of the iconic modern-era *Boeing 747 Jumbo Jet*. The "Brab" was intended to only carry around 100 passengers in luxury far removed from the "knees under your chin" discomfort of modern short haul jets, a busy 747, Boeing's latest *Dreamliner* or even the mighty twin deck *Airbus 380*. Cabin bedrooms were to be installed for long transatlantic flights, something that had until then only been seen on the great airships, alongside luxuries like a cocktail bar, set to attract wealthy travellers used to the luxury of ocean liners. This plane was a heavy beast, and it was no surprise, on its first test flight, when it slowly lifted off a specially lengthened runway that the test pilot Bill Pegg remarked with upper class understated astonishment: "It works!"

Sadly, the *Bristol Brabazon* was ahead of its time, among other things, too large for most of the airfields and terminals that existed, and too expensive for the airlines to buy and put into service. Reluctantly the government, which had subsidised the development costs, pulled the plug on the project before the plane got to the production line stage. Though it is pleasing to record that some of the innovative technology developed by the project did, at least, help make the *Bristol Britannia* commercial airliner, a post-war success. That showboating flight over Glasgow I witnessed – intended to impress the taxpayers who were footing the bill – was not the only time the "Brab" took to the Scottish air: The famously long Prestwick runway came in handy for test flights. On one such trip the huge aircraft ran into a flock of Ayrshire starlings and, after a few scary minutes for the crew, it landed smeared in feathers and blood. Those great propellers had kept turning. The decision to end the project was a sad conclusion to the dream of the far-sighted Lord Brabazon of Tara. After spending millions on his "baby", it ended up being sold for a few thousand pounds for scrap. One link with the *Bristol Brabazon* remains in Scotland at the Museum of Flight at East Fortune (more of this magnificent place later in this book). Part of the massive undercarriage that once supported the weight of the plane, said to be three times heavier than any previous airliner, sits on display: a poignant if realistically inadequate reminder of a dream that died.

Much of this book looks many years further back into the early history of flight in Scotland and beyond, but the "Brab" was a sort of literary sparking plug for me. Until that day, along with my early teenage school friends and encouraged by my father, I had mostly been fascinated by stories of the legendary liners, freighters, mighty oil tankers and warships built in the many yards on Clydeside. The gleaming silver plane, which growled its way across the sky rather elegantly, but slowly by the standards of today, watched by adult and child alike in anxious admiration, was a different sort of giant. Now stories of aviation shared my attention with the exploits of the transatlantic liners racing across the pond in search of the legendary Blue Riband. It is somewhat ironic that those luxurious liners were to be swept into history by the *Brabazon*'s more successful intercontinental successors of the jet age, that could get you to America in a few hours rather than a week.

That dreich day in King's Park was the start of a compelling journey into the past. Long before airliners, some supersonic, crossed the Atlantic daily and American stealth bombers flew in secrecy into the NATO airbase at Machrihanish, sparking newspaper reports of flying saucers, pioneers of aviation were at work in the unlikely surroundings of places like Kelvingrove Park in Glasgow's still elegant West End. And in many parts of

Scotland, from great industrial cities to remote islands, pioneer aviators played a more important role in the world history of flight than is often acknowledged. This book makes no claim to be comprehensive or academic. It is just one enthusiast's idiosyncratic look at the story of some of the experimenters, pilots, planes and airfields of former times in Scotland. If your favourite airfield, aviation personality or tale is not here, my apologies – apart from anything, to tell it all in detail would be to destroy too many trees and it would need the lifting capacity of a jumbo jet freighter to move the paperwork around!

1

The Hawk, the Bat and a Near Miss with World Fame

Almost everyone and their granny – as Glaswegians like to say – is aware of the Wright brothers and their flights, at Kitty Hawk on a remote North Carolina beach in 1903. Fêted as the first sustained powered controlled flight, it etched the name of a couple of bicycle mechanics from Ohio into world history. The first flight was piloted by Orville which lasted around twelve seconds and covered 120 feet. The Wrights made four flights that day and the last, piloted by Wilbur, was the more impressive. This time their flimsy craft of wood and canvas was aloft for almost a minute and covered 852 feet. And, as they say, the rest is history. Much less famous than the American pioneers is a former Royal Navy man with strong Scottish connections called Percy Pilcher. Aviation buffs apart, it is fair many Scots are unaware of how close he came to beating the Wright brothers to the finishing line of eternal fame. He could have been first by the lengthy period of three years. Even fewer are aware of the part Scotland, particularly the fashionable Byres Road and Kelvingrove Park in Glasgow's elegant west end, played in the development of flying machines that changed the world. But for an air tragedy more than 100 years ago it could all have been so different.

Like the Wright brothers Pilcher had an engineering background. Though not a Scot – he was born in Bath in 1866 – he spent long periods of his working life in the country. He served in the Royal Navy for several uneventful years as a midshipman before taking work as an apprentice in the Govan Shipyard of Randolph, Elder and Company. It seems that in Scotland the young Englishman first developed his thirst for innovation and invention and his passion for flying. It is perhaps significant that John Elder himself was a pioneer in marine engines helping to speed the transition from sail to steam. In addition, Elder and his company was one of the first to see the advantages of "production line" engineering, later to be exploited and developed by Henry Ford. Elder was, it seems, way ahead of his time, a real forward thinker. Working in this, at the time state-of-the-art shipyard, must have been stimulating for the young Pilcher. Elders eventually became Fairfield's, builders of some of the most famous warships and passenger liners in the age of steam. It had many changes of ownership down the years, latterly becoming part of the huge BAE Systems organisation which helped build Britain's latest super aircraft carriers *HMS Queen Elizabeth* and *HMS Prince of Wales*. Despite the fact that Elders was unusually innovative, I fancy that Percy Pilcher could never have imagined the day would come when fast jet powered aircraft would scream off the flight deck of such a ship as "Big Lizzie", as the crew call her, and her sister carrier. However, Pilcher was clearly aware of the effect of wind on canvas and the notion that it could be converted into lift that would take some form of man-carrying flying craft off the ground.

Around the world many others were also taking an interest in "soaring machines". These early pioneers often hoisted themselves into the air on what were basically large kites, pulled aloft by teams of horses, local strongmen, relatives or assistants to the designers. In Pilcher's case his family helped provide the muscle power. The success of early hang-gliders proved the possibility of the notion that such devices could one day be powered by petrol engines. Some pioneers even dickered with the dead-end route of weighty steam-powered engines. In particular Percy's sister Ella and a cousin, Dorothy, helped him with research and construction, even piloting his early gliders when he lived in lodgings in Glasgow's now trendy Byres Road. There is a folk tale in the area that Pilcher had to move from the Byres Road nest to a less busy street nearby because his landlord thought he spent more time than he should cluttering up Kelvingrove Park mucking around with kites. It is perhaps more likely that the owner of the flat was fed up with it being used as an "aircraft factory". If this were true it would have been unusual in this part of Glasgow with its bohemian atmosphere. Far more normal would have been a tenant being asked to leave because he was spending too much time in the famous Byres Road howff, The Curlers, rather than in the park.

The search for the secrets of flight were being sought in mainland Europe and America as well as in Britain. Many pioneers of early flight corresponded with each other, exchanging theories and data, and sometimes travelled long distances to meet. This cooperation is impressive – the Wright Brothers were aware of what was happening in their field of research in Europe as well as the work and common experience of fellow Americans, Augustus Herring and Octave Chanute especially. Chanute was a highly qualified engineer with expertise in truss systems used in the design of bridges, which was of great help in fabricating flying machines. His experiments near Lake Michigan were of interest to the Wright brothers. Alongside their correspondence it has been claimed that some of his ideas were used by Pilcher, although presumably the latter's experience of sailing ships and building steam-powered vessels were also a significant help in his aviation ambitions.

The first machine Pilcher flew (in 1895) was called the *Bat*. Ella helped build this contraption of bamboo, wire and fibre. He first tested it at Auchensail, near Cardross, making him (it is claimed) the first person in Britain to make repeated unpowered flights. Later that year he met Otto Lilienthal, a German who was ahead of most in the field of developing piloted gliders. They put their heads together, eagerly uniting efforts in the fight to escape from the earth to the skies. When Pilcher got back to Glasgow he built two more hang-gliders, the *Beetle* and the *Gull* based on what he had learned from the meeting with Lilienthal. This was a world where all sorts of crazy and not so crazy ideas were swapped around by experimenters, and bravery was part of the mix in flying from day one. There is a remarkable archive photograph of a pilot, apparently Pilcher's cousin Dorothy, hanging from one of his gliders in 1897. This courageous pioneer looks to be fashionably dressed in a skirt with no sign of a crash helmet and certainly no safety belt!

You wonder if this use of females as pilots had anything to do with the advantage a light weight combined with a sureness of touch might bring, as all the early innovators faced the same problem of getting extra lift without adding too much weight. The way ahead in the early days was bi-planes or triplanes, though simply adding an extra wing was useless until further lift could compensate for extra weight. Another wing or two also brought construction problems. Speeds were slow in hang-gliders which were often towed like kites, and the heights achieved low. Anyone who has watched old documentaries of multi-wing craft will have seen shots of them collapsing spectacularly in a heap of wood and canvas and the pilot, if lucky, pulling themselves out of the wreckage and limping off back to the drawing board. But a dive into the ground from forty feet in a flimsy fabric and wood contraption could also kill as surely as hitting an inconvenient mountain top in a fast jet. A fact that both Lilienthal and Pilcher would eventually demonstrate by dying in accidents when their gliders stalled and fell to the ground.

During these years of experimentation in flying machines Pilcher also had a successful academic career – after Elders, he was an assistant lecturer to a professor of marine engineering and naval architecture at Glasgow University, handy for tests in Kelvingrove Park. But in 1896 he resigned to go back south as an assistant to Hiram Maxim, the famous inventor of the automatic machine gun. Maxim was American born but moved to the UK at the age of forty-one, continuing a remarkable career as an inventor, even taking out a patent on a mouse trap! History does not seem to record how successful it was, but certainly his early efforts at powered flight were useful if not significantly fruitful. Like all inventors Maxim was often stretched for funds to turn his ideas into something solid. Oddly one invention, a fairground ride called the "Captive Flying Machine" did make money which he used to help fund experiments with the real thing.

Pilcher's most successful machine, the *Hawk*, was built in Scotland but never flown here. Perhaps also the most famous of Pilcher's gliders, it is now on display in the Atrium of the National Museum of Scotland in Edinburgh. It was originally constructed in Glasgow near Kelvingrove Park, where it underwent some testing by Percy and his sister. With a wingspan of around eight metres, it weighs over twenty-two kilos. Pilcher had found a way to create a little "oil" engine, thought perhaps light enough to be carried into the air and power a propeller, converting a glider into a powered flying machine. The National Museum is a splendid place to spend time in, but gazing up at the flying machine itself, it is hard to imagine that such an unlikely looking object was the beginning of a path that would lead to a massive aircraft like the *Airbus 380*. An interesting footnote is that the legendary scientist Lord Kelvin, who knew the Pilcher family, was not a proponent of powered flight and teasingly warned the inventor that "he would certainly break his neck" which was sadly prophetic. But it was a jocular and kindly criticism, as Kelvin still gave Percy and Ella space in the University of Glasgow to use as a base for their experiments.

It was on his return to England that Pilcher made perhaps his most famous flight. In 1897, he broke the world distance record, flying more than 800 feet in the grounds of Stanford Hall in Leicestershire. By that time, it was obvious that the future of aeronautics was one of powered flight rather than simply impressing folk with the ability to glide around a few feet above the grass in the breeze, fun but of little practical value. It was on that same ground, two years later that the Pilcher story came to a tragic end. The cost of all Pilcher's early experiments had put him in debt and whilst these days crowd funding would be the answer, what Pilcher needed, and quickly, was well-heeled sponsors. He had planned to demonstrate his latest model, a triplane, to wealthy potential backers on an autumn day in 1899, but a few days before the flight he had trouble with the little 4hp engine and despite wind and rain on the day, he took the fateful decision to fly in his *Hawk* glider rather than disappoint those who had turned up at Stanford Hall. When in the air a breakage occurred on the framework, he was thrown to the ground from a mere thirty feet. He suffered severe injuries and he died two days later. His triplane was never flown publicly in his lifetime. He was only aged thirty-two. And, as they say, the rest is history. Well, maybe not quite. There was a fascinating twist in the Pilcher story to come more than a hundred years after his death.

Aviation historians in the early years of this century, on re-examining Pilcher's design for the triplane, concluded that it might have worked. In 2003 the BBC television series *Horizon* came up with the idea of seeing how close Pilcher had come to the dream of being the first true aviator to conquer the dream of sustained controlled powered flight. The BBC commissioned the School of Aeronautics at Cranfield University to investigate Pilcher's work, which included building a replica of the triplane (with modern material and some safety measures). Piloted by an aircraft designer, Bill Brookes, this machine managed sustained controlled flight for one minute and twenty-five seconds compared with the Wrights' fifty-nine seconds. Point made. "If only . . ." is a much used and abused phrase, but it is unavoidable in this context. The story of aviation might have been completely changed and aviation history rewritten if only Percy Pilcher had not taken the fateful risk of attempting a flight on that rainy and windy day in 1899. That "if" is important. Death ended his dream.

Most of the great advances in science, technology, medicine and astronomy have from time to time been surrounded by claim and counter claim about "Who did it first?". Radio transmission, the development of television, and notably the regular squabbles about Nobel Prizes, are cases in point. The achievements of such as the Wright brothers, Marconi and Logie Baird have generally risen above rivals. Though it is important how the question "Who was first?" is defined. Logie

Baird is a good example – he did transmit moving pictures, but the method he devised was a long way from that used in the modern smart TV. Social media has made the world a smaller place and through it, toiling out of the public eye in some obscure country, you can now find at a click, folk who claim to have been the first and unrecognised by the mainstream in whatever their field was. So too, with the development of aviation – inventors and innovators working apart from each other often come up with the same idea. It's inevitable that some dispute the belief that Pilcher could have been the only pioneer to challenge the Wrights. Though the evidence of that 2003 BBC reconstruction seems to leave little room for argument. So I was surprised to read in one of my favourite monthly publications, the *Scots Magazine*, that in 1953, rather than Percy Pilcher being the man who could have beaten the famous Ohio bicycle makers to the winning line, another Scot – Preston Watson had been the first flyer to actually do it. Though the claim did seem largely anecdotal, a bit suspect and was not made by Watson himself. Watson's younger brother had also made this claim in an article for the then *Manchester Guardian*. Even back then there seemed to my mind no convincing evidence to prove this sensational claim. Much of the so-called evidence seemed well-minded hearsay. Indeed, today the body of aviation historians in Scotland have dismissed the claim out of hand.

The suggestion that Preston Watson was first to achieve proper sustained controlled flight over a distance, put about by others rather than himself, looks, from afar, something of a shame since it obscured some of his genuine innovations. Watson, a Dundonian, did provide some interesting ideas on how to control a plane in flight and deserves his place in history. His idea that a small wing mounted on an A-frame above the main wing could provide lateral control, sounds to the layman rather like just moving the rudder forward, but nonetheless it was used with apparent success in three planes built between 1909 and 1913. Preston Watson was notable, too, in that in 1915 he gained his Royal Aero Club Certificate number 1,117. He had been a student at a flying school operating out of Hendon, London's aerodrome, as airports were called at the time. Before this he had sought a commission with the Royal Naval Air Service. Sadly, the little-known early flier died in an accident in 1915 not long after gaining that licence. It seems that no pilot error was involved as reports said the aircraft he was flying disintegrated in mid-air over Sussex. His body was taken north more than 500 miles to the Western Cemetery in Dundee.

It is fascinating, if not surprising, to note the connection between shipbuilding, especially in Scotland, and the development of aircraft. Similarly to Pilcher, Richard Harold Barnwell was a pioneer with strong Scottish connections – he was educated at Fettes in Edinburgh and his father was a director at a Clyde yard. Along with his younger brother Frank, Harold built a form of glider in Stirlingshire in 1905. In 1906 the brothers were running a garage business in Causewayhead where they built three planes between 1908 and 1910. The first failed and crashed on test, but the next effort was a success. Unlike many claims of flight which, according to one, perhaps cynical, historian I spoke to, consisted of a lucky bounce or two over a bumpy grass strip that launched the test craft a couple of feet in the air before a swift return to terra firma, there is no doubt that the Barnwells' effort took to the air. This was Scotland's first powered flight in July 1909. The plane was piloted by Harold and took off from a field near the Wallace Monument, travelling eighty yards at around twelve or thirteen feet high (no oxygen masks needed there). It ended in a crash, but since many a pilot's definition of a good landing is one you walk away from, it must be considered a success. The brothers' third attempt, this time flying a monoplane, was a tad more impressive. In January 1911, unseasonable fair weather gave the Barnwells an opportunity to win a prize of £50 offered by the Scottish Aeronautical Society for the first flight of more than a mile to be made in Scotland.

Later that year the brothers moved south and Harold gained his pilot's licence. Around this time there was plenty of scope for adventurous young men, and they were mostly men, to attend one of the many flying schools that were springing up in England. Brooklands' famous banked motor racing circuit had plenty of space in the infield areas of the track. Brooklands School of Flying was one of the most esteemed of these establishments and it was here that Harold Barnwell got the coveted slip of paper, Number 278, that officially made him a pilot. Though it would be more appropriate to say that he earned his wings the day he took to the air and flew around in the shadow of the Wallace Monument back in Scotland.

Brooklands was more than just a flying school or racetrack. From the early years it was a centre for test flying, the actual construction and design of aircraft. Some say it was the most significant site in the development in aviation . . . an astonishing 18,600 new aircraft of more than 250 types were built, assembled and tested in the many flying schools based at Brooklands. Harold Barnwell first studied flying at the Bristol school but later joined the Vickers Flying school as an instructor and was quickly one of the best. He even helped Noel Pemberton-Billing win a bet with Frederick Handley Page that he could get his licence in just one day. A remarkable man, Barnwell then became Vickers' chief test pilot. Clearly a bit of a rebel, in 1915 he designed and built his own *Barnwell Bullet* without the knowledge of his employers, from the company's own parts stores. This ended badly for the pioneer with the machine wrecked on its first test flight.

However, the Vickers firm kept him in employment as a test pilot, then a more dangerous occupation than now, and he lost his life testing a new fighter a couple of years later. His significance in advancing aviation is marked by memorials in Causewayhead and Balfron. Nonetheless, the obvious, and natural connection, between ground-based engineering enterprise and the march of aviation from primitive hang-gliders to powered flight is demonstrated in the careers of such as the Barnwell brothers and Pilcher.

A lesser-known Scot, Andrew Baird is another example of a flier with engineering in his background. He was the son of a fisherman and was apprenticed to a blacksmith in his native Galloway. But, showing the restlessness of many a young man, he moved on to a spell as a lighthouse keeper on the island of Lismore, near Oban, before getting employment in the iron works at Gartcosh in the Central Belt. He then settled down on Bute where in 1887, at the age of twenty-five, he started a black-smithing business and married. It seems unlikely, considering he was based in a fairly remote island, but he became fascinated by the exploits of the early fliers. Perhaps a visit to an Aviation Week down south in Blackpool was the spark. Whatever the inspiration, he did get in touch with Louis Blériot and S. F. Cody seeking information on building a flying machine of his own design. The Baird Monoplane seems to have been built in similar design to the one which Blériot used in his 1909 cross-channel flight. Though there were some detailed differences. It had a small four-cylinder water-cooled engine made for him by an Edinburgh firm. As a blacksmith he had no problem with the bodywork. In the same manner Percy Pilcher had found, bringing the family into the project helped; Baird had his wife sew the silk fabric that covered the wings. On completion the plane was shipped across the holiday island of Bute from Rothesay by horse and cart to the beauty spot of Ettrick, on the west coast. I can testify, from frequent visits camping there with my southside Glasgow scout troop, that this looks a tempting site for a test flight. Plenty of flat fields and smooth sand, facing into the west winds.

The Baird story becomes a bit puzzling from then on. The plane's test flight took place in September 1910, some months after that of Harold Barnwell. An observer from *Flight* magazine was on the island and reports say the plane took off over the sand but suddenly veered from its path and crash landed. How far and how high it flew was not recorded with any detailed evidence. But it seems certain that the time in the air was short. Baird, however, certainly made a mark in the early history of flying – his one craft was on show before the test flight. It is claimed by some sources that Sir Thomas Sopwith the famous aircraft builder used some of Baird's ideas, but I have seen no solid evidence of this. Sopwith's *Camel* was built in significant numbers and served Britain well in the First World War, meaning a blacksmith from Bute may have helped to alter history. A Scottish registered charity was established to: Celebrate the achievements of Andrew Blain Baird, a son of Bute who histori-cally achieved the "First Attempted All-Scottish heavier-than-air powered flight" in September 1910 in a flying machine of his own construction. Although the word attempted is significant.

*The Hawk can be seen in the National Museum in Edinburgh and there is a *Bat* replica in Glasgow's spectacular Riverside Museum. There is also a monument at Stanford Hall close to the point where Pilcher received fatal injuries in the Hawk crash.

2

Some Air Show – The Planes Came by Train

A day out at an air show now is an entertaining and informative jaunt for families, attracting vast crowds, though it must be said that these days low flying screaming jets can be difficult for toddlers or the family pet to endure. Ear plugs should be sold along with the tickets. But noise was hardly the main problem at Scotland's first air show, remarkably held as early as 1910, only a decade or so after Percy Pilcher died when the Hawk dived to earth. The frail wood and fabric craft that thrilled the crowds at Lanark who had travelled from all over lowland Scotland to watch the seventeen "stringbags" (a surprising number of entries for the time) flying over the suitably flat and pleasantly green sward of Lanark racecourse. These craft, a mesmerising sight to the spectators, mostly merely puttered quietly, and relatively slowly, a few hundred feet above ground. The displays went on for several days, an amazing sight just a year after Blériot had stunned Europe by conquering the English Channel in a plane that was the first to be fully controlled by the partnership of a cockpit joystick and a foot-activated rudder, a combination that still is in use today. That air shows were even contemplated so soon after the exploits of the early experimenters is an impressive example of the rate of progress in the early days of flying. Some sources say 250,000 found their way to Lanark racecourse and there is even speculation the Baird of Bute mentioned earlier was among them. The choice of the pleasant little Lanark racecourse as the site for that historic air show was, as the saying goes, a "no brainer". Long, well-conditioned stretches of relatively flat grass runways were available, as were turnstiles normally used to admit locals bent on subsidising the lifestyle of the heavily tweeded bookmaking fraternity. There was good access from road and rail from Edinburgh and Glasgow and heavily populated nearby industrial Lanarkshire. And as a bonus the stables could be used as hangars. The Caledonian Railway Company had even built a station on the racecourse doorstep and many of the modern flying machines were transported to it by old-fashioned steam trains.

A few months before Scotland's first air show there had been a similar event in the south of England, notable for a crash that killed Charles Rolls of Rolls-Royce fame. Rolls had been a pioneer balloonist and became acquainted with the Wright brothers, soon realising there was more to flying than being pushed hither and thither by the wind. He bought a *Wright Flyer* and made a number of successful flights but died when his plane broke up in mid-air at an air display at Bournemouth. From the Rolls crash on to the present-day air shows have been dangerous (the 2015 Shoreham disaster is a timely reminder when a *Hawker Hunter* display crashed, killing eleven people and injuring eighteen others). What had happened in Bournemouth was taken on board by the organisers at Lanark and no plane could fly closer than 300 yards from the spectators.

In another wee bit of aviation history Lanark was the first time when planes were accurately timed over a mile-long course allowing world records to be set, including awards for both speed and altitude. There were no fatalities and the aviation press (yes, there was such a thing even then) hailed the meeting as a great success. One wonders what King William I (died 1214) who reputedly founded the course would have thought of the happenings in the skies above Lanark that week in 1910. Racing ceased in Lanark in 1977 owing to financial difficulties, something many a punter over the years could sympathise with. Some remnants of the old course can still be seen today. And in early 2019 one of the many TV antiques shows so popular these days turned up a couple of gold medals awarded to competitors at the show. One was the prize for altitude with the winner reaching between six and seven thousand feet! Not much of an altitude these days when commercial airliners often exceed 40,000 feet, but still they valued much lower than I would have thought, only at a few hundred pounds.

3

When Pigs did Fly, and the Capital was Bombed

You are cruising along at not much more than a hundred miles an hour at a few thousand feet on a dark, cloudy and icy night, patrolling shipping lanes and searching for submarines in the Eastern Approaches during the First World War. Without warning one of the engines stutters to a stop. You are in real trouble. A mechanic must crawl outside the relative warmth and safety of the body of your flying machine and, hanging on for his life, he must stretch out over flimsy struts and wires to reach the ailing engine and find out what's the problem. If you are lucky he diagnoses the fault and, in the howling cold of the slipstream, manages to fix it and crawl back inside the cabin of his "blimp". The patrol restarts. This is life on a British airship in the First World War.

A brave Scot was at the heart of it. The hundredth anniversary in November 2018 of the end of the First World War, and the founding of the Royal Air Force, was a trigger for the retelling of much heroism and tragedy on land, sea and air in the press and on TV. The remarkable career of one Scottish aviation pioneer was belatedly highlighted in a splendid little exhibition that toured west coast libraries – Major James Gardner Struthers. As a Flight Commander of one of Britain's small fleet of "blimps" he successfully searched for, found and attacked no fewer than seven German submarines threatening British marine traffic with the potential to disrupt supplies and kill hundreds of seamen. For his life-saving service in the air he was awarded the Distinguished Flying Cross by King George V on October 2, 1917. Major Struthers was said to have accumulated more flying hours than any other British airship pilot.

The exhibition featuring his career was collated by Eleanor McKay, Bibliographic and Local Studies librarian, at Live Argyll, after meetings with Major Struthers' son Charles. It is hoped that his grandson Archie will set aside display space in the family home at Ardmaddy Estate near Oban for the many fascinating items held in the family collection, including photographs of great historic value taken by the air ace himself. Among other artefacts available to go on display are airship banners, gas goggles and propellers, even some wreckage from a shot-down *Zeppelin*, though whether it came from one of the German airships that once attacked Edinburgh isn't clear.

This was the nasty side of the airship story. The dream might have been flying passenger "liners" of the air floating graciously across continents as the wealthy sipped fine wines as the ground, or sea, a few thousand feet below them slipped past. But the fact is that this very low-speed form of travel made airships ideal for bomb raids on civilian targets. The airmen who flew such craft could lean out of a window and drop a bomb by hand with a good chance of hitting the target. These early bombs were a way behind the precision bombing raids of the RAF on Germany in the Second World War, but they could kill the luckless folk down below and damage or destroy enemy factories. The Clydebank Blitz over two nights in March 1941 is beyond doubt the most horrific air attack in Scotland's history and the story of this appalling event is told in more detail later in this book. But these infamous spring nights in World War Two were far from the first German air assault on the country.

Around twenty-three years earlier, during the closing stages of World War One, the growing use of bombing for the air was becoming more and more deadly using fixed wing aircraft and the lighter than air "gasbags". This time the bombs did not drop out of the bomb bays of sophisticated and highly powered Luftwaffe bombers but were thrown to the ground by the crew from the gondolas that hung beneath the giant German airships, generically known as *Zeppelins*. (This book is mainly concerned with powered aircraft and airships, but it is interesting to note that a year after Montgolfier's Paris success in taking to the air in a balloon in 1783 a Fifer who became known as "Balloon" Tytler became the first Briton to make a successful ascent though not all his attempts were completely successful – his final flight ended with a crash in front of hundreds of paying spectators in Edinburgh). *Zeppelins* were first used as a weapon of war in Britain in raids in 1915 on Great Yarmouth and King's Lynn south of the border. The following year Scotland was a target. The attack, like that on Clydebank, was intended to damage a docks area, this time at Rosyth and Royal Naval ships anchored in the Firth of Forth to guard against naval attack from across the North Sea. The *Zeppelins* were slow and difficult to manoeuvre, particularly in bad weather. This was to hinder the later development of the craft as long-distance passenger carriers in peacetime.

In war, though the lack of speed could be useful for bomb-aimers in the right conditions, it could also create a tragic lottery on where the bombs fell. It was thought that three airships were intended to be involved in the foray into Scotland in 1916, but one turned back, perhaps because of navigational or mechanical problems, and another also got lost and bombed empty fields in the north of England. The other also appeared unable to navigate successfully to Rosyth and turned instead inland in a search for targets.

The airships were huge lumbering targets slowly and visibly edging north, but there were few effective anti-aircraft guns around our cities and towns at that time. It was easy to see where the airships were heading, but there was little the civilians on the ground could do but wait and watch for the bombs to fall. Scotland's first air raid began on a Sunday evening in April. Twenty-four bombs hit Leith and Edinburgh in less than an hour killing thirteen people and injuring twenty-four. Ian Brown of the National Museum of Flight at East Fortune in East Lothian has been quoted as saying, "The idea was to destroy property and set fire to them and cause civilian casualties. Basically, their aim was a terror attack." The same reasoning that prevailed in 1941 in Clydebank. The bombs were a mixture of incendiaries and explosives. One early bomb hit a tenement and the occupants had a lucky escape – an explosive went through the ceiling and down four floors without injuring anyone. Another bomb exploded near Edinburgh Castle, though no one is sure if it was the target. It is interesting to speculate on whether the Forth Rail Bridge would still be intact if that airship had reached Rosyth.

Airship development continued in the years after the Great War. In the 1930s the latest gigantic German airships such as the *Graf Zeppelin* and *Hindenburg* were glamorous objects that made the headlines around the world. Their successes, like a safe return trip from Europe to Rio, were unthinkable for the fixed wing aircraft of the time. These huge structures filled with inflammable gas and powered by primitive engines, dangling from their immense bodies, were the first aircraft to have the word luxurious attached to them. Airships in this golden age looked to be the future of aviation – both as deadly bombers dropping explosives on unprotected cities AND as "airliners" which ambled slowly across the great oceans transporting an adventurous and wealthy elite sipping champagne, the best brandies, wines and enjoying fine dining which matched that of the great hotels of the day. The airship dream had been spawned as far back as the late 1890s. The most important of the early experimenters in rigid airship, rather than the balloon, was the German Count Ferdinand von Zeppelin whose name latterly gained usage as a term for all airships based on his designs.

But the belief that airships would become as numerous as ocean liners and freighters largely ended in the awesome fire and explosion of the *Hindenburg* as it tried to land in bad weather at its mooring mast at Lakenhurst near New York on May 6, 1937. Of the ninety-seven on board thirty-six died. There have been many aircraft disasters that took a greater toll of life. But few incidents altered the development of air travel in the way the demise of the *Hindenburg* did. (The British *R101* disaster is another.) Minutes before it burst into flames the *Hindenburg* had been filmed flying high serenely, seemingly safe and indestructible, above the skyscrapers of New York. Hundreds of thousands watched its progress as it headed for the mooring mast. Mooring an airship was a primitive exercise involving aircrew throwing ropes to be caught by teams of workers on the ground. Live radio broadcasts covered the totally unexpected and sickening fiery end of the *Hindenburg* at Lakenhurst. Reporters, photographers and the crowds who had flocked to the airfield itself to welcome this magnificent flying machine burst into screams and tears as the flames spread through the structure, its stern falling to the ground leaving the bow still high in the air. Huge clouds of smoke and flame swirled across the airfield.

Epitomising the emotion and shock of all who saw the crash was the famous outburst by an anguished and tearful newsreel commentator, "Oh the humanity". Passengers were burned to death in the airship itself, others died leaping out and their falling bodies were caught by the cameras. One ground handler also died. These photographic images, some of the most famous ever taken, live forever in the memories of those who viewed them.

The image of the airship in the public mind became that of a fiery death. The dream was over. What had happened? Like the assassination of John F. Kennedy, theories tumbled throughout the media and scientific journals for years after the disaster. Sabotage was a popular theory. To the layman the most potent and accepted explanation is that a spark ignited the inflammable gas used to lift the airship off the ground. Or set fire to the fabric of the airship itself. What caused the spark? That is still controversial. The death throes of the airship age did, however, tend to overshadow their early success and the fact that, particularly for Britain, they saved lives as well as killing them. Sadly, the role, both defensive and offensive, that airships and Scotland played seems to have largely drifted out of most of the histories of "the war to end all wars".

It is ironic that today the thousands who travel from Glasgow's International Airport fly almost directly above one of the most important sites of airship development – William Beardmore and Company's Inchinnan Airship Construction Station. Beardmore's was one of the most significant companies in the history of engineering in Scotland. Its range of activities was spectacular, ranging from such mundane products as taxis, cars and motorbikes to shipbuilding, manufacturing railway engines, diesel engines, conventional fixed wing aircraft, armour and guns for Royal Navy ships and airships. The company's history is inexorably linked with the legendary Parkhead Forge (now a shopping centre) in the east end of Glasgow. The forge was established as far back as 1837 by the Reoch Brothers and four years later Robert Napier, a dominant figure in the history of Clyde shipbuilding, bought it to make forgings and iron plates for warship construction in his new yard in Govan. But this early enterprise ran into financial bother and William Beardmore Snr, then based south of the border, was called in as a partner to rescue the Forge and moved north with various members of his family.

Eventually William Jnr became the sole partner, founding William Beardmore and Company in 1886. Within a decade the works spread out over twenty-five acres and for a time was the largest steelworks in Scotland and a major player in the booming shipbuilding industry on both banks of the Clyde from Glasgow city centre to the Tail of the Bank off Greenock and Port Glasgow. The aviation connection started in 1913 when the company bought the British manufacturing rights of *Austro-Daimler* aircraft engines. This enterprise soon expanded to the building of actual planes at a facility in Dalmuir down the river. Aircraft manufacturing was no little sideline for the company; it was a major enterprise, the scale of which was demonstrated by production figures. One of the first models built was the illustrious *Sopwith Pup* (built under licence at Dalmuir) and a later version designed for aircraft carrier use – a hundred of these planes were delivered to the fledgling Royal Naval Air Service. This was a great success although a following craft, the *Nieuport 12*, also built under licence, was less fortunate. Beardmore incorporated many refinements into this plane which delayed production so much that by the time they were ready for service they were virtually obsolete and used mainly for aircrew training. Some were never used, left to rot or were cannibalised for repairs. Beardmore continued to experiment with an early flying boat and tri-motor transport for the Royal Air Force, at the same time churning out a long list of airplane engines for other manufacturers.

One engine, the *Tornado* (a name much fancied in the aviation industry) was used in perhaps another of the most famous disasters of the airship age – the loss of the *R101*. One of the Scottish-built engines of this ill-fated "gasbag" was on display in the Science Museum in London. The huge airship was the largest flying object yet built when it was "walked out" from its hanger, hauled along by hundreds of ground crewmen hanging on to ropes, at Cardington in Bedfordshire in 1929. It was such a sight that it is said that more than a million people travelled to the field to see it floating tethered to its mast, a remarkable engineering construction. A sensation of the age. But it all ended in tears after another tragic fiery accident that killed forty-eight people (more than had died on the *Hindenburg*) including the air minister who had masterminded the project, Lord Thomson, and other government figures, when in poor weather it hit a ridge near Beauvais in the autumn of 1930. As in most accidents it was a combination of circumstances, on this occasion including tricky weather conditions and the blind refusal of the political and aviation elite of the time to accept the evidence of the test flying programme that much was amiss in the design and manufacture of this experimental flying machine. When it crashed it was en route to India on what was purely a propaganda mission. Airships were vital to the expansion of the British Empire, with their ability to transport large numbers of passengers and large volumes of freight to the furthest red-coloured corners of the globe. Ready or not, the *R101* took to the skies. That it only managed a few miles across the channel was a deadly blow to both aviation and British politics.

4

Paisley Gas Bags, Dambusters and a Stowaway

Beardmore had constructed its own airships (*R27, R32, R34, R36*) at a factory near Paisley around the end of World War One. However, the *R101* story provides insight into the development of such craft now largely forgotten (other than by aviation buffs), though there have been some recent attempts to develop hybrid aircraft and airships built in England in hopes that the use of new technology will allow such craft to realise the early promise of heavy lift slow flying vehicles. First: the size – it was 731 feet long, a length only surpassed by the *Hindenburg* which took to the air seven years later.

No doubt today's *Boeing 747*s and the *Airbus 380* are impressive, but they could not compete with the planned luxury of the *R101*. It was initially designed to cater for around 200 passengers and forty crew with two decks inside the envelope. The plan also included promenade decks with windows and a dining room in which formally dressed waiters could ply sixty passengers with fine wines and haute cuisine. There were to be fifty passenger cabins, some to accommodate four people. And in the ultimate irony, considering the fact that many who flew in airships died in fireballs, there was even an asbestos-lined smoking room! (Maybe not so surprising when up to a decade or so ago some airline pilots smoked in the cockpit.) Clearly there were folk who believed that the concept of airships could change the world.

Among the famous names involved in the era of airships were two remarkable men – the *R100*, a rival experimental project to the *R101*, had a design team headed by Barnes Wallis that included Nevil Shute Norway as a stress engineer. Wallis went on to be famous for inventing the bouncing bomb used by the Dambusters in the Second World War (he also worked on the *Wellington* bomber), and Norway became a famous novelist under the name Nevil Shute. In his autobiography, published in the 1950s, Shute highlighted contrasts in the rival projects – he saw the *R100* as essentially a conservative design and the *R101* as more of an experimental leap and over-optimistic, though he later modified his criticisms. As mentioned earlier, the airships were vital to binding the British Empire together with their ability to conquer long distances. The two different designs were intended to compete in a search to find the best solution to take the concept forward. On the face of it the *R100* succeeded as it made a successful Atlantic crossing in the summer of 1930. But after the *R101* disaster a few months later the plug was pulled on the Imperial Airship Scheme and the *R100* broken up for scrap.

Perhaps some of the dangerous optimism surrounding the scheme had been fuelled by the relative success of airships built by Beardmore at the Inchinnan Airship Constructional Station on land near what is now Glasgow International Airport. During the First World War the Admiralty had given the company a contract to build airships and work started on the site in 1916. It was labour intensive and there were said to be difficulties in getting workers to this "isolated" site. Ironically there is now a motorway and rail line a few hundreds of yards from the location. However, a hundred years or so ago the solution was to build fifty-two houses known as the Beardmore Cottages on the doorstep of a giant hanger (similar in size to the famous airship shed as Cardington). Four airships were built before the contract was cancelled in 1919 and the station closed in the autumn of 1922. The giant airship shed and other buildings were demolished and there is little for any passengers passing overhead in a jet climbing out of Glasgow International to see to remind them of a piece of aviation history.

Of the airships built at Inchinnan the most famous was the *R34*. It was stationed at East Fortune airfield near Edinburgh for a time and in 1919 flew from there to Long Island, New York, on the first direct flight from Britain to the United States. On board were eight officers and twenty-three men (one a stowaway) and a kitten called "Wopsie" who had been smuggled aboard as a mascot. According to *The London Times* report of the flight, the human stowaway was an airman called Ballantine. Apparently, he came out of his hiding place six hours after the giant airship had left Scotland. He had originally been on the crew list but had been taken off shortly before take-off in order to save weight and had sneaked back on board. The newspaper report said that he told American reporters "Look at me. Do I look like an extra load?" and went on to say: "I made up my mind to go anyhow. I stowed away between gasbags six and seven intending to stay there till the end of the trip. But I became sick and delirious and had to give myself up." The crew looked after him and in a couple of days he was fit enough to work his passage to New York. He said that the commander Major

Scott had not spoken to him, but he expected he would. And the major did indeed have a word, telling him he would not be on the return flight and adding that a court martial was on the cards, though the officer remarked: "I don't expect he will be subjected to any very severe punishment."

One of the fellow officers on the trip was a Major Pritchard who has an interesting claim to fame: he was at that moment the first person from Europe to travel by air and land on American soil. It came about because the landing party had little experience of dealing with large airships and the bold major had to parachute to the ground to take control. The transatlantic journey made history, but the East Fortune airship connection was ending. The *R34* made just a few more flights and on one was damaged in a storm after it had contacted a Yorkshire base, trying to get home after a North Sea patrol. It was scrapped. The East Lothian airship station was closed in February 1920 though it continued as a base for fixed wing activity. The future was not cumbersome giant airships, but smaller and faster jets.

The skies above Paisley and Edinburgh were not the only places where airships were to be seen floating serenely and silently below the cloud cover, an awesome sight to catch the attention of earthbound folk. South of Aberdeen there is a heavily forested area around Longside. Now, viewed from either the air or the ground, there is nothing to tell you that this was the site of the most northerly airship station in mainland Britain – RNAS Longside. In the closing years of the First World War the need for patrols to watch for enemy activity in the North Sea shipping lanes was identified. This was the ideal job for airships (even after the demise of the giants of the era, smaller "blimps" continue to do such surveillance work in many parts of the world, right up to the present day). Construction of the north-eastern base began in 1915 and when complete it operated until 1920. Post-war the many large buildings which comprised it were torn down and forestry planted, obliterating almost all trace of the enterprise. The snag at RNAS Longside was much the same as operating airships worldwide – they were difficult to control in bad weather, particularly in strong winds, often a feature of the north east weather of Scotland. So along with the base itself there was a small mooring facility at Montrose to be used when getting back to Aberdeen was a problem. As all Scots know the Doric spoken under the northern lights of old Aberdeen is at times unintelligible to those of the lowlands. And the northerners were not fazed when technology posed a challenge. To them the airships were knows as "Lenobo Soos" – an inventive combination of the name of the site and the local dialect for a pig. So, don't let anyone ever tell you pigs can't fly. They did at Longside!

5

Was it a Boat, Was it a Plane? A Strange Story . . .

Beardmore's involvement in multiple industries such as steel making, shipbuilding and aviation is far from being the only example of overlap of activities of companies in Scotland during the massive advance of technology in the last century. One of the great names in shipbuilding, William Denny and Brothers, is another example of a company at the leading edge in one field expanding its expertise and desire to innovate into another field. It is often said that "Glasgow made the Clyde and the Clyde made Glasgow" but downriver from the city lies Dumbarton and there a slightly different version of the old saying is still remembered: "Denny's made Dumbarton and Dumbarton made Denny's". Same difference as the Scots say! The ship most associated with the yard at the foot of Dumbarton Rock, where the Leven joins the Clyde at the end of its journey from Loch Lomond, is the legendary *Cutty Sark*, though others built there also made a mark on history, including the famous American riverboat the *Delta Queen* and the ill-fated *Princess*

Victoria, which sank, taking more than 100 lives in the winter of 1953, in a massive storm on the Irish Sea.

The castle on the rock, a volcanic plug that dominates the scenery for miles on both banks of the great river, has been a stronghold since the Iron Age and it is even said that Merlin the wizard of Arthurian legend once slept there, as did Mary Queen of Scots (is there a castle in the land where it is claimed she never laid her head?) Of more relevance to this book is the fact that ship repairing is recorded there as far back as 1515, centuries before the Denny family set up their yard in 1844 and built around 1,500 ships before closure in 1963. There is now a fascinating little museum on the site and in it a remarkable model of what, if the technology had been around at the time, could have been a successful helicopter. The design was based on a ship's propeller and on the correct assumption that if a propeller could push a vessel through the ocean, then stood on its head, it could haul an "airship" upwards. The snag was that this was in the era when steam was just replacing sail and engines powerful enough to whirl giant helicopter blades at several thousand revolutions a minute were many years in the future. But it did show that even then backroom guys at Denny's could think "out of the box". Particularly Edwin Mumford the head of the shipyard's famous Experimental Tank, which was mostly used to improve the design of ships' hulls.

Eventually Denny's went on to build the famous hovercraft and sea planes. The family name is still held in high regard in the town, perhaps because the pioneering spirit seemed to flow thought the genes and down the decades. One of the founders, William Denny, was even way ahead of his time in his treatment of his workers. While many of his shipbuilding rivals exploited their workers with the zeal of a Victorian mine owner getting his workers to dig for black gold in a hunt for profit, he provided his with decent housing. And there were happy days under one of his successors, Maurice, whose workers enjoyed picnics and sports days out and winter party evenings when such things were generally unheard of in the hard grind of the soulless factories emerging in the new technological age. In Denny's what is now called "human resources" was admirable. In contrast, the hovercraft, now a largely forgotten part of the yard's story, was not one of unqualified success. For a while the invention of a craft that could skim a few feet above water, land, or swampland, would be a game changer in the transport world. Said to have been invented with the aid of old coffee cans, this vehicle used an engine to suck air from under its hull and contain it within a rubber skirt, floating the craft on the cushion of air whilst forward motion was achieved by propellers. Was it a plane, was it a ship? Take your pick. In my view there is no satisfactory answer other than to acknowledge it was a hybrid. The puzzle on how to describe it even caused confusion in London where for a while, one Denny's hovercraft briefly served as a passenger carrier on the Thames.

In 1960, a new Air Navigation Order officially classified the hovercraft as aircraft, meaning the *Denny D2 Hoverbus* needed a permit to "fly" on the Thames. But there was still confusion on whether it should follow maritime rules or the laws for flying machines – even though it never got to an altitude other than a few feet. The legal complications even caused ructions in the august newsroom of the *London Times*. The story of the new navigation order was written, interestingly, by a reporter with the rather old-fashioned title of Aeronautical Correspondent, not the Shipping Correspondent. On the face of it the hovercraft was ideal for use on the Thames or the Clyde and the Firth of Clyde. Fast and capable of "flying" unhindered by choppy seas, it looked as if it would sweep the world. But it never happened.

What held it back was one of the problems that doomed the *Concorde*, yet unlike the beautiful, but ultimately failed, supersonic jet it was not a sonic boom. It was simply that the hovercraft was horrifically noisy to operate, as anyone who travelled in the large versions used on the England-France cross-channel ferry routes would confirm. Even smaller versions were so noisy that on rivers in cities and other crowded areas the populace at large turned against them. There were also problems with the "skirt" that contained the cushion of air and generally maintenance was too high. Still, the hovercraft continues to have military value in operations where noise is not too disadvantageous. But it is largely a footnote in the story of Dumbarton. Not so the yard's aviation adventures.

The connection with flying never approached the achievement of the Denny's yard in launching more than 1,000 ships but is nonetheless hugely impressive, though not locked in the local memory so securely as that of shipbuilding. As far back as 1906 two of the Denny design staff, Edwin Mumford and J. Pollock Brown, had designed a heavier than air machine based on research into ships' propellers. Like today's aero modellers these two innovative thinkers realised that light material such as bamboo and in the case of the model makers, Balsa wood, would be advantageous. But both these materials had major defects – they were easily destructible. Wood was extensively used in pioneering aircraft manufacture and even the famous World War Two fighter, the *Mosquito*, was basically wooden panels glued together. The early Denny craft had a bamboo frame, light enough until water in the form of rain or spray was absorbed into it, making it totally unsuitable. This craft was destroyed in a storm in 1909 then rebuilt using aluminium, the way ahead in air frames, but it too was destroyed when it was hit by a gale on tow back to the yard after making a successful hop of around 100 yards at an "altitude" of ten feet. This was in 1914 and in the coming years, the "war to end all wars" also ended that experiment.

After the end of the First World War, The Blackburn Aeroplane & Motor Company in Brough, Yorkshire, which had been making "flying machines" as early as 1908 prospered, as it became clear in the 1930s that flying was no longer to be simply weaponised with primitive bi-planes and tri-planes flying above the trenches and making the occasional bombing raid on civilians. The aviation industry had burgeoned. Commercial aviation was on an astonishing growth path with technology developing at a remarkable rate, opening the world in a way never seen before. But with all this activity came the realisation that the looming war would need bombers and fighters in massive numbers. The Air Ministry was aware that many of the plants needed to build the planes were concentrated in England and manufacturing capacity needed to be more widely spread throughout Britain, including to Scotland and Northern Ireland. The Clydeside area was ideal since there was a huge available workforce of men – and in the early days it was mostly men, though when the actual fighting started women – who had engineering skills and a background in factory work – were recruited in large numbers and played an important role in keeping production going.

Sir Maurice Denny, the yard's Managing Director, had been among industrialists who had founded the Scottish Flying Club at Renfrew in the late 1920s and interestingly, saw flying boats as a natural successor to passenger shipping and thus a threat to shipbuilding. Indeed, he at one time had plans for flying boat bases in newly built harbours in Scotland. This was in the days of the *Empire Flying Boats* opening up Africa from Britain and the great *Boeing 314 Clippers* plying pacific routes. The yard had also dickered with an early form of helicopter as mentioned earlier and built aircraft for the Royal Flying Corps in the First World War. In short, he was the ideal man with the ideal company to do a deal with Blackburn and start manufacturing in Scotland. He got into correspondence with Robert Blackburn himself, who already had several military aircraft contracts and was a noted pioneer of early aviation. The men became friends, fellow enthusiasts in the development of flying, and a joint company was formed and a factory in Dumbarton built.

The site at the foot of the famous rock was a natural one for seaplanes but, as it was fairly distant from any airfield, there was a problem in moving land-based aircraft around. Denny suggested a solution that was no surprise to anyone who knew this innovative thinker – barges constructed by the shipbuilding section to move partially stripped down, newly completed planes upriver to the Royal Naval airfield at Abbotsinch, later to become Glasgow International. This could accommodate the new *Botha* bomber and, of course, a factory on the banks of a wide river like the Clyde, sitting downriver as the Firth opened, was ideal for the new experimental top-secret *B20* sea plane, which despite several successful innovations never went into mass production. Still, two years before the start of the Second World War a new company called Drumbrough was established and training for production was under way. The purpose-built factory showed even in such turbulent times Sir Maurice's instinct to go the extra mile for the workers (4,000 of them at peak) in that there was a good canteen and even a small theatre.

In America the concept of the factory town had taken grip and something similar was happening here thousands of miles across the Atlantic. The aircraft building complex had its own fire brigade, ambulance and police services and, naturally, a Home Guard, which must have been a far more efficient bunch than that portrayed in that wonderful TV comedy *Dad's Army*. As production took a surge upwards in 1939 it became obvious that one of the ideas behind the building of such a large new enterprise near Glasgow was seen to have been understated – the workforce needed by the new enterprise required much more than folk from its doorstep. A recruitment campaign brought workers from Fife, the Highlands and Islands (including such unlikely places as Gigha and Skye) and even Edinburgh, Glasgow's great rival, to mingle with local ex-shipyard workers and Yorkshire men on the factory "production lines", building planes for the war effort. This was a time, too, when women in large numbers joined the workforce, many in their early twenties and teens. It was an exciting time for folk who had never strayed far from their own hearths. The women were even told to keep an eye open for Nazi spies trying to infiltrate with the workers and send the secrets of the new planes back to Germany. It was hard and exciting work but liberating. Lifelong friendships were created and many a good time was had at the end of the day. It is remarkable that the grainy black and white photographs of the workforce show so many smiling faces. Especially when during the Nazi raids on Clydebank and Dumbarton the workers huddled down on the factory floor, fingers crossed that the next bomb was not the one that would kill them, while searchlights pierced the blackout darkness and air raid sirens wailed in that fearsome way that no one who lived through the Blitz will ever forget.

In 1996 Alan M. Sherry produced a first-class booklet which tells of an interview in which one of the young female workforce describes the thrill of witnessing the first flight of the huge *Sunderland* flying boat which was the major design built, rather than the *B20*, and how it trundled slowly down a small concrete landing slip, then taxied down the river at what seemed reckless speed before the throttles were fully opened and it finally hauled itself into the sky to climb and bank away from its birthplace, soaring over Dumbarton. The *Sunderland* was an extremely large, powerful and heavy aircraft and the Clyde authorities were worried about the wash created by its take-off run damaging the walls of the carefully dredged shipping channel. Consequently, on completion the *Sunderlands* were towed downriver to a base at Rhu on Gareloch. So that take-off flight from the immediate surroundings of the factory was not an everyday occurrence. It was good PR to let the workers see what they had collectively produced finally take the air, although the girls were not too impressed with the gift given to them to mark the great day – a packet of cigarettes.

Although the Blackburn factory produced many different types of plane with great success, including the *Botha* bomber and others, the *Sunderland* was perhaps the most famous. Its nickname was "The Flying Porcupine" because it bristled with armaments. It was said to be much feared by German fliers who happened to encounter one out on a submarine hunt. I suspect U-boat captains were also unhappy about catching sight of one in the skies. As early in war as 1940 the *Sunderland* chalked up its first unassisted U-Boat kill. Produced in its hundreds between 1941 and 1945 it took part in the Berlin Airlift and was still flying during the Korean War, with some surviving planes converted to passenger use in remote parts of the globe where lakes and wide rivers outnumbered airfields. This is hardly surprising since the design was based on the pre-World War Two commercial *Empire* flying boats.

What is surprising to the modern air traveller, used to flying "knees under the chin" in cramped modern jets is, however, the level of luxury these lumbering "ships of the air" provided. The size and weight (around eighteen tonnes) and its huge tail plane which looked to the workers in Dumbarton as high as a local tenement, made it the *Jumbo* of its day. There were large cabins fitted with seats or bunks and a decent sized galley and dining area giving something of the luxury expected by people who would normally travel in the latest liners. To add to the nautical ambiance, the huge cockpit was referred to by the crew as the "bridge". These flights were operated by Imperial Airways and a crew of five and just under twenty passengers was the norm. The *Empire* class opened Asia, Africa and Australia up to the moneyed classes of the time. The machines themselves were large enough to have two decks, allowing for the creation of a spacious promenade cabin where passengers could stretch out their wealthy legs and chat during the long journey.

Unlike modern aircraft it went into service with few problems and, indeed, when the production line had settled down, the planes rolling off it were simply given a single test flight and handed over to the customers, which included Qantas. The wartime *Sunderland* which emerged from the original design, but without the extra weight of passengers, wine stewards and butlers, had plenty of room for huge fuel tanks that allowed maritime patrols of up to fourteen hours and plenty of room for bombs, mines and depth charges. In its final wartime configuration, it also had a searchlight, the latest versions of radar and an astrodome. The *Sunderland* was a common sight around the Clyde and Gareloch and the denizens of Oban, the ferry gateway to the Highlands and Islands, were familiar with its great size and the roar of its four Bristol Pegasus radial engines as it flew in and out of RAF Oban, a flying boat base built on the island of Kerrera across the bay from the town. On the mainland facing the island lies the beautiful Ganavan Sands area where the RAF had a wartime Flying Boat Maintenance Unit. These days the beaches are thronged in the summer with tourists sunbathing (when they can) and enjoying sea swims, often from the relative luxury of nearby caravans. Not much remains to be seen of the RAF days, at Ganavan or Kerrera, though there is a memorial at Ganavan Bay and a good museum in Oban itself.

Though the Second World War was the *Sunderland*'s glory days, the Scottish flying boat connection began in the early 1930s when the RAF scoured the Scottish coast for places suitable as bases for flying boats like the *Supermarine Stranraer*, *Saro Lerwick* and latterly the *Sunderland*, then growing in popularity especially in the luxury section of passenger craft. Kerrera island just off the west coast was judged suitable for refueling and servicing and a slip and jetty were constructed. The base became operational in 1938 and by 1940 was home to the RAF's 210 Squadron's *Sunderlands*. When it was operational some of the many fine hotels facing Oban Bay became billets for the servicemen. I wonder if any of the holidaymakers who now frequent these busy and popular places ever give a thought to their wartime history. Cromarty Firth was also deemed suitable as a base for these large and majestic looking aircraft, though they were slow and cumbersome albeit providing comfortable long-distance travel on patrol or in passenger configuration.

I never sampled the luxury of travel in an *Empire* or *Sunderland* craft which were true flying "boats" rather than the modern smaller float or seaplane. But in recent times the enterprising Loch Lomond Seaplanes company provided service to and from Oban by air from Glasgow. Their small float planes even, for a while, took off from the Clyde itself as well as from their base on the loch near Balloch. The possible danger from floating debris on the take-off run on the river, almost in the city centre, curtailed this, but I can say after experiencing it that a flight taking off and landing on one of the most famous lochs in the world is memorable. Seen from the air the mountains of the Scottish Highlands and Islands provide vistas as wondrous as any in the world. This was also confirmed with a flight to the now under-exploited little airstrip at Broadford on Skye. The early part of my flight was conducted in beautiful sunshine with magnificent views inland to the lush farms of Perthshire, the Cairngorms and the Hebrides to the west. But Scotland being Scotland, the approach to Skye was conducted in a storm accompanied by the rat-a-tat of hail bouncing noisily off the fuselage. The pilot was unfazed by the racket and we were soon on the ground waiting for a taxi to take us to Portree and a "freebie" cruise on a Cunard liner, tough work but someone had to do it.

Possibly the most important passenger a *Sunderland* carried was the Duke of Kent, the younger brother of the then reigning king, George VI. He left the Cromarty Firth base in a *Sunderland* (Flight W-4206) on 25 August 1942. Popular, he and his wife Princess Marina had a few weeks previously celebrated the birth of a son. Adjectives like gallant and handsome were thrown about when this man, who was an Air Commodore, was discussed in newspapers and drawing rooms. But that was very much an outsider's perception. This Royal may not have been as squeaky clean as was thought at the time. There were, in high society, allegations of drug use and sexual impropriety. The destination of his secret mission was Iceland. Wild rumours abound, even one that Rudolph Hess, Hitler's deputy, was on board the *Sunderland*. I can find no evidence that he was on the *Sunderland* and to me the real mystery is how many crackpot mysteries seem to surround the Fuhrer's deputy's life. However, the truth of what happened on Flight W-4206 causing it to end in a fireball on a remote Highland hillside will never be known – sabotage, pilot error, a Nazi plot, drinking, who knows? A final touch to this intriguing mystery is that one survivor was allegedly silenced by the RAF and died many years later taking any secrets he had kept to the grave.

Back down in Dumbarton the factory area which contained the aircraft factory itself has long been cleared and swept away. Now there is a tidy little football stadium in which Dumbarton FC play. The club's old home was aptly called Boghead and was infamous among supporters, away teams and visiting football scribes for its tendency to be quickly turned into muddy mush. Around the new home of the club which does not seem to have the defect of the old there is currently little sign of the area's importance in aviation history, although the Denny ship museum half a mile or so inland is a remarkable place and well worth a visit. But where the old factory stood there is almost nothing to remind you of it or folk who worked there. Alan's book telling the story of Blackburn Aircraft Company's factory, like the shipyard, located at the foot of Dumbarton Rock, includes a little anecdote of visiting a housing scheme on the edge of the town where two of the streets were named Sunderland and Blackburn, English names not expected in a Scottish town. He spoke to local kids including teenagers on the streets asking if they knew why such names had been chosen. "Sorry, mac, nae idea" seemed the most popular response. The *Short Sunderland Flying Boat* and the *Blackburn Botha* bomber had been built on a site at Denny's – and their contribution to victory in the Second World War had passed out of folk memory. Despite both Denny and Blackburn having had many connections with the early years of flight, that slipway down which the *Sunderland* trundled to go to war is rather weed strewn and empty.

6

Travelling to Work in Your Own Autogyro

In the early years of the twentieth century the industrial west of Scotland seemed awash with major innovators in engineering, shipbuilding, steel making and the manufacturer of locomotives in the age of steam. Railway works in Springburn and Polmadie in Glasgow employed thousands. It is staggering to consider that North British Locomotive Company in Polmadie alone employed 8,000 people in 1907. These works, and others, built engines for emerging railways round the world. As a youngster I remember watching the impressive sight of these huge locos being lifted, by equally impressive powerful dockside cranes on the Clyde, on to the decks of freighters which would take them to the far-flung corners of the globe. The list of recorded destinations is truly formidable, including: Canada, Newfoundland, Argentina, Paraguay, France, Spain, Angola, Gold Coast, Kenya, Uganda, Tanzania, Malawi, Rhodesia, South Africa, Egypt, Palestine, India, Ceylon, China, Japan, Malaysia, Philippines, Australia, and New Zealand. In shipbuilding circles "Clyde built" was a guarantee of quality. "Polmadie" or "Springburn built" does not have quite the same ring worldwide, but the years of service these railway engines put in should have earned them a similar slogan to that of the great ships.

Not far from the loco works at Polmadie lies the factory of marine engineers George and James Weir in Cathcart. It was also a massive employer, and further proof of the ability of such as Beardmore, Denny and the Weirs themselves, to step out of any niche field and ride the wave of creative innovation. It is fascinating for example to note that both Denny and the Weirs stepped out of the box, as it were, to experiment with non-mainstream concepts such as helicopters, hovercraft in Denny's case and the autogyro in the Weirs' case. Not for them the gentle "evolution by tweaks" in the design of fixed wing flying machines. These were giant leaps of invention and imagination. Sadly, the Weirs do not seem to have been given the same acknowledgement of their aviation successes as others. Nor does it seem widely recognised how important the firm's role in the Great War was. Anyone anywhere with an interest in engineering knows the fame the company achieved in the specialised area of building pumps for ships and latterly its desalination products and general engineering expertise. Less well known is that Weirs were involved in the production of more than a thousand aircraft for the First World War. Also largely forgotten by the general public, is the role G & J Weir's Cathcart factory played in the development of the helicopter. Which is odd since the family was at the heart of aviation progress and experimentation for years. Including a leading role in the creation of the RAF itself.

Viscount Trenchard is often given the title "Father of the Royal Air Force", but a couple of Scots also had much to do with the creation of the air arm of our military forces. One was

William Weir who was a friend of both Lloyd George, Winston Churchill and David Henderson, a most remarkable polymath. In fact Trenchard is on record as saying Henderson was the real father of "the boys in blue", a view supported by noted aviation historian Dugald Cameron. Henderson, born in 1862, studied engineering under Lord Kelvin in Glasgow. He was not a man to be pigeonholed, as his subsequent career showed, and after university he joined the Argyll and Sutherland Highlanders, later becoming Lord Kitchener's spymaster during the Boer war. He was also an excellent pianist and composer, setting some of Kipling's poems to music and he used his engineering skills to help him design theatrical sets. On the face of it an unlikely aviation pioneer. But Henderson, always an inquisitive mind, followed the progress of flight under the Wright Brothers, realising the potential of their primitive flying machines as military weapons. His ideas found little favour with the military elite, more interested in training their horses and having their uniforms ironed and their leather polished. Undeterred he took flying lessons himself at the late age of forty-nine and was found to be a "natural". Gradually coming to their senses, the Government formed a committee to look at the future of air power with Henderson as one of a three-man group which led the way to a military air service. The Royal Flying Corps was formed in 1912 and the word "squadron" brought into use. This was remarkably soon after the events in Kitty Hawk in faraway North Carolina. Maybe the early resistance to Henderson and his ideas was not quite as entrenched as it seems.

At the start of the First World War a squadron of Flying Corps planes had gone south from Montrose to cross to France. Henderson also went across the channel to be the commander of our air forces. At the end of the war, amid much politicking, Henderson and Rothermere resigned from what was known as the Air Council on the day the Royal Air Force was born (April 1, 1918). This opened the way for William Weir, a Churchill favourite, to come on to the scene. As mentioned, the family firm G & J Weir had built complete aircraft for the war, without profit, something that Churchill appreciated, and he put William Weir in charge of aircraft production. With Rothermere's resignation he became Secretary of State for Air and was ennobled as Lord Weir of Eastwood. It was Weir who was given the task of appointing Hugh Trenchard as leader of the RAF. Trenchard was a member of the awkward squad with an arrogant streak and not too keen on the job, but he was given an offer, as they say, that he could not refuse. So started the RAF. And so started a remarkable peacetime career for William Weir, a man who was a leading developer of the auto-gyro which led to the successful development of the helicopter and a man ahead of his time in backing the ideas of Frank Whittle, the jet engine pioneer when conventional engineers had no faith in the concept. When Weir first became interested in rotary wing flight, pioneers were using the term "helicopter" to describe craft both hauled into the air and pushed forward by powered rotors. The big snag here, and it always tended to harm the development of such machines, is that engine failure would inevitably cause a crash. The possibility of gliding to a landing was zero. Juan de la Cierva, a Spanish aristocrat, seemed to have a solution to the problem – a "plane" that was pulled forward by an engine driving a propeller, causing a flow of air to spin a rotary "wing" which provide lift.

In its modern form it worked, as devotees of the *James Bond* movies will attest. The Farnborough Air show was in existence as far back as 1925 and it was the place chosen by Cierva to show his invention to the world. In the crowds watching the demonstration flights that day was James G Weir who was impressed and rang his brother William to enthusiastically endorse the autogyro, as it became known, as the way ahead. Lord Weir himself was so enamoured by Cierva's ideas that he wrote to Henry Ford with a notion to get the car maker involved in mass production. Left to his own devices Henry Ford might just have started an aircraft building revolution, but his son Edsel, a controversial figure who some suspect was not the smartest spanner in the toolbox, turned the idea down. Left on their own Weirs eventually became involved in the autogyro project in 1932. At this time Cierva's organisation was in trouble and the Weirs too were feeling the effects of the worldwide depression which was hitting shipbuilding and in turn the industry's suppliers.

It says much for the forward thinking of the Weirs that even at this low point they had the foresight to acquire the rights to produce an autogyro of their own design. It emerged the next year, a tiny fifteen-foot long machine, designated the *W1*. To enable a take-off and set the rotors speeding needed the assistance of a muscular ground crew of helpers pulling on a rope, in the fashion of a mackerel-basher starting an outboard. Despite this, Cierva, who died in a passenger air crash in 1938, would have approved of the developments which now allowed the autogyro to jump directly into the air without a take-off run, something that was the key to real success for helicopters and spelled the end of the autogyro itself, though a few still thrill air show spectators. Various versions appeared in the next couple of years sometimes tested at Abbotsinch, later to become Glasgow International Airport. How far ahead of their times the Weirs were is proven by the tales that in the late thirties they could commute from their Ayrshire mansion in Dalrymple to a field in the then undeveloped Thornliebank area, near the Cathcart factory. Eventually, the arrival of the Second World War, and the national pressure to increase aircraft production to take on the Luftwaffe, saw the company put the autogyro and future helicopter era on hold. This left the field open to the Americans and to this day the name Sikorsky would win you a pint in a pub quiz on the invention of the helicopter. A shame really. Various versions of the Weir autogyros can be seen in air museums, and there are still some homegrown fun machines around, but if you want to see one of the Weir models in flight your best bet is to catch a showing of the 1935 film version of John Buchan's *The Thirty-Nine Steps* where one is shown in a chase scene flying over the heather.

The story of the early development of rotary wing aviation, and its commercial use in Scotland, highlights the vital role such machines played in the exploitation of North Sea oil. Indeed, without the helicopter, oil extraction (i.e. getting at the liquid gold under the waves) would not have had the colossal effect on the country's economy it had, though sadly that effect is slowly declining. What went on in suburban Cathcart in Glasgow way back in the thirties links the Weir family with events almost 100 years later. To get a flavour of what it is like to be part of the modern oil industry and the use of helicopters almost the way we use buses, as a convenient way to go to work, I spoke to a highly experienced North Sea saturation diver, Ray Bulloch. He describes it in an interview for my book *Scotland's Cruel Sea*:

What can you say about helicopters? Call them "Choppers", "Paraffin Budgies" and "Whirlybirds" – whatever you like – they're still noisy, cold and uncomfortable. They vary and some are better than others; however, they have become the transport workhorse for offshore installation personnel, and for good reason. Their arrival and departure on any offshore installation never goes unnoticed and is always commented on, whether you're getting on it, or I should say hoping to get on it, cause you're never sure till you're strapped in and off, or just counting the number of times it'll come and go before you are getting on it.

The first time I was in a helicopter in the early seventies, I found it quite exhilarating, and even though that exhilaration waned, it never entirely disappeared. That may well be due to the attitude towards safety in those days, which compared to modern practices, was very lax. That relatively laissez faire attitude engendered a relaxed 'get a window seat and peer out of the window' type feeling, which bitter experience was later to change. In the early days you just turned up and got on (some passengers even with a hangover and certainly worse for wear from the night before); none of the stringent safety measures which apply now were in operation. These days they won't even allow you on if you're overweight.

The novelty of helicopter flight would give way to a resignation that we would have to put up with the noise and discomfort of what could well be a long flight. Conversation was all but impossible and dozing or reading was the easiest way to pass the time. Flying from onshore, the view from the window, if you had one, would be of the heliport falling away below you and the experience of rising over the surrounding countryside or urban area, depending on where you were flying from. The edge of a city like Aberdeen or an island north of the mainland would all eventually give way to the vast expanse of the ocean. I remember reading somewhere that the Earth is a 'rocky little planet'; however, it's hard to believe that when you fly over many miles and miles of water for such a long time. When you're on an offshore installation it has an aura of power, of being solid and immovable; however, when you're flying towards it on a helicopter and see it from the air, set in the context of the North Sea, it looks so insignificant and you can readily understand why some of the platforms are lost to the sea they stand in. It gives you perspective.

A minority of passengers, however, find helicopter flight harrowing and are very nervous before and during the flight and, I suppose, given that helicopters can and do fail, they have a point. Most people believe, of course, that it'll never happen to them and being at the time a saturation diver, I'm sure I believed it even more so.

All of the above is of course weather-dependent as helicopters are susceptible to all sorts of weather delays ... "W.O.W." (waiting on weather) used to be the usual term. If you were offshore, you could be "fogged in", stuck on the installation till the weather cleared. If you had been counting how many "get ups" until it was your "get up and go", you were constantly scanning the weather and when on your crew change day a WOW notice appears your heart sinks, especially if it's an occasion when there is something special you want to attend to on shore. Not everyone felt the same though – some guys want the extra money and don't mind being "fogged in"; for them it's "money mist".

Even worse, imagine it's a couple of days to Christmas and your crew change day has come and gone, you're praying for the weather to clear just enough to let the chopper land. You get told by the diving superintendent the chopper's on its way and to go and get changed and packed. You go and you're packed in literally two minutes because you've been ninety-five per cent packed and ready for a week. You've sprinted up to the radio control room and you're waiting impatiently for the "Budgie" to land, which you hear it is about to do, when, at the very last minute, in walks some company person and they take your place. It's not their crew change day for another day or so but they're not taking any chances with the weather, so they're taking your place and they're off early for Christmas. You're stuck until "whenever", which is what Control usually tells you if you make an enquiry about the next chopper. It happens!

It's the opposite when you're still ashore and "WOWed"; then, hopefully, you're staying in a good hotel and getting paid for the privilege, though in my experience it's more often the former than the latter! However, for all the bad points and disappointments of offshore helicopter travel, it's hard to see any other practical way of delivering offshore personnel to and from installations. Ship to rig transfer via the "Billy Pugh" is not for the faint-hearted. It may sound odd, but I rather enjoyed it . . . but that'll be the "It'll never happen to me" attitude again.

Ray added an interesting footnote on recent changes which are a remarkable contrast to the turn up and go ethos of the old days. Now you need proof that you have been scheduled for a visit to an offshore location. If you are going offshore, the following is compulsory:

- Valid passport or identity card;
- Valid medical (offshore) certificate;
- Successfully completed basic Introduction to Offshore Safety course and Emergency Response Training (0.5A) including Helicopter Underwater Escape Training (HUET), or:
- Basic safety certificate (such as VCA, MIST, or another equivalent certificate issued in another country).

- You are not allowed to bring hazardous substances, alcoholic beverages, narcotic drugs, or arms of any kind onto the offshore platform.
- Your luggage will be checked for such items.

Upon arrival at your offshore destination:

- Unfasten your 4-point harness after arrival when prompted by the crew or HLO (Helicopter Landing Officer).
- Never open the door of the helicopter yourself, always let the crew or HLO do that.
- The HDA (Helideck Assistant) will unload your luggage and place it next to the helicopter.
- When prompted by the HLO, exit the helicopter and pick up your luggage. Freight will be unloaded and taken off the helideck by the HDA.
- Leave the helideck as instructed by the HLO.
- As soon as you are below deck, you can take off your life jacket and hand it to waiting passengers or the HDA.
- Always first report to the radio or control room, which is signposted, possibly only with arrows.
- You will subsequently be given video instructions regarding health, safety, and environment (HSE). You are under obligation to adhere to these instructions.
- Also make sure you are familiar with and abide by safety instructions and the code of conduct for the platform.

It is a comprehensive list and recent accidents have led to an even more serious attitude to safety developing. But you suspect that in the future, despite all the good intentions of the authorities, it could happen again. The history of North Sea helicopter ferry flights is littered with accounts of what went wrong and good intentions that never seemed quite enough. Initially the public was not particularly aware of the situation, but any complacency was quickly swept away by a series of headline grabbing accidents.

Perhaps the most significant of these in the early days was when a *Boeing 234LR Chinook* plunged into the sea on approach to Sumburgh Airport in the Shetland Islands on November 6, 1986; forty-seven including the crew were on board and only two survived. On the face of it the *Chinook* looked an ideal vehicle for serving the rigs. A tandem-rotored, twin engine, medium-lift helicopter, it had been in service with the RAF for four years before this accident. The primary design was for military applications and it was remarkably successful in this role, being considered rugged and reliable. During the Falklands War there were even reports that one *Chinook* had carried eighty fully equipped troops on a mission. Even more impressive is the claim that during the Gulf War one aircraft transported 110 Iraqi prisoners of war. But even the military record of this legendary "whirlybird" is flawed.

In June 1994, an RAF aircraft was taking a group of twenty-five British intelligence experts and a crew of four from Belfast to Inverness for a conference when it came down in poor visibility on the Mull of Kintyre. No one survived. Controversy and intrigue went on for years as to the cause, and it is still controversial. The crew were initially unfairly blamed, but many experts believed they were scapegoats and that the disaster had other causes. Rumblings of all sorts went on for years including accusations of sabotage. Eventually that harsh decision on the pilots by the authorities was overturned and the crew cleared. But what really happened is still far from clear. This was the RAF's worst disaster since the Second World War. It is a murky story.

The Sumburgh disaster shocked Scotland and brought home the human price of cheap oil. The civilian version of the *Chinook* had, like its military equivalents, a reputation as a workhorse. The details of the final hours of the *Chinook* that crashed in 1986 demonstrate that well. It had originally operated out of Aberdeen airport but a few days before the crash had moved to Sumburgh to fly a shuttle service to the Brent oilfield. Its first flight that day had been delayed by an oil leak, but that was repaired, and it left the islands at around nine in the morning to visit three platforms with freight and passengers. After a mere hour and a half, it took off from the Brent Platform C to head home. Its height for most of the journey was around 2,500 feet but as the airport came into view it was cleared to descend to 1,000 feet. The intention was to land on runway twenty-four. But at around four and a half miles out the airwaves went silent.

As the crash was happening a coastguard search and rescue helicopter had taken off from Sumburgh and its crew spotted life rafts in the sea. One survivor was seen clinging to a fair-sized bit of floating wreckage. The crew managed to winch him to safety and as they did, they saw another survivor amid a group of floating bodies and he too was plucked to safety. Despite desperate searching no more survivors were found. Early next morning a search for the sunken wreckage was begun by a diving support vessel, but it struggled to hold its position at the site because of rough seas and powerful currents. Fortunately another vessel Shell Expro's *Stadive* soon arrived on the scene and it, a semi-submersible, was able to handle the conditions well enough to recover the cockpit voice recorder, some of the fuselage, rotors, rotor heads and control systems which were shipped to the mainland for accident investigators to examine. The *Stadive* also managed to recover all the bodies of the victims bar one.

The cockpit voice recorder revealed that the crew had noticed a rise in the noise heard on the flight deck followed by an ominous loud bang. This was the sound of the rotor blades colliding when they lost synchronisation. The official report said the accident was caused by this happening owing to the failure of a "bevel ring gear" in the forward transmission which had been modified. The underlying blame was put on the "inadequacy of a previously accepted test programme and the failure of a stringent inspection programme". The usual raft of recommendations to prevent a similar disaster followed. Basically, there was to be much tighter inspections control on modified components. A review of the procedures regarding Automatically Deployable Location Transmitters was to be reviewed as the beacon on the *Chinook* failed to work when it suffered impact damage. This was the swansong of *Chinooks* in the North Sea oil industry. They were withdrawn and sold to be used in other parts of the world utilising their heavy lift capability but not licensed for passengers. The oil industry took the decision that basically the *Chinooks* were too large for offshore supply work. Something that anyone who had seen one of these noisy giants at an air show or perhaps parked at an RAF base, might have realised before lives were lost. Mechanical failure was to blame for this accident but when you see film of a huge *Chinook* landing on a tiny platform in a storm it is obvious that only the great skill of the pilots prevented many another disaster.

The other great controversial shuttle airbus to the rigs to force its name onto the front pages of Scotland's newspapers was the *Super Puma*. It has a chequered career of major incidents and loss of lives. But occasionally it has been at the centre of a good news story and Bristow's Flight 56c between Aberdeen and the Brae Alpha rig back in midwinter 1995 was one such tale. The difference between life and death on this occasion was largely due to pilot skill. The commander of the copter, Cedric Roberts, was massively experienced with almost 10,000 flying hours in his logbook and the man in the right-hand seat Lionel Sole was likewise a chopper veteran who had been flying with Bristow for five years. On a routine trip the *Super Puma* flew into bad weather and was struck by lightning. The bolt damaged the tail rotor and although the aircraft managed to stagger along for a few minutes eventually the rotor failed completely, and the pilots had to make an emergency rotation onto the rough sea. This was done so skilfully that all eighteen on board (sixteen passengers and crew) were able to exit the aircraft onto a life raft and were rescued. The investigation found fault with the design of the rotors, making them prone to damage by lightning strikes. It is not surprising that half a century of oil and gas exploration and extraction, which meant that at times there were almost 300 rigs out at sea to be serviced, led to a great many accidents. But that brush with death on Flight 56C was not the only lucky escape. Seven years before, a *Sikorsky S-61N* was forced to ditch when travelling from a drilling rig seventy miles offshore. All passengers and crew – thirteen people – were saved. On that occasion luck was with them as the accident occurred in almost perfect weather conditions. Helicopters can land in the sea but for the occupants to survive, the weather and sea conditions are the main factor between life and death. In a similar accident to that which occurred to the *S-61N* some years later, twelve men died of hypothermia, that deadly factor in the waters around Scotland. This crash occurred in December when the sea was at its coldest.

The oil industry accidents are too numerous for all of them to be discussed in detail here, though in *Scotland's Cruel Sea* some of the other tragedies and the causes are examined. But one curious statistic emerges – up until the 1990s the accident rates in the Norwegian and the Scottish sectors were roughly similar, but from then on the safety record of the British fields dropped behind that of the Scandinavians. I have seen no solid evidence of any one reason for this odd statistic. But maybe some would point to the *Super Puma* and its record. Maybe it was simply that the North Sea was perhaps the most crowded helicopter air space in the world.

7

The Wee Toon, the Space Shuttle and Aliens

As a long time, part-time resident of Argyll, I can set my clock (almost!) twice a day, morning and evening, to the sound of a gentle purring in the sky a thousand feet or so above my garden in Carradale. It's the regular daily Glasgow/Campbeltown flight, on approach low over Campbeltown to Machrihanish airport. It's a vital and reliable connection between what the locals call the "wee toon" at the tip of the Kintyre peninsula and Scotland's biggest industrial city. The *Twin Otter* often used by Loganair these days is not what you could really call an "airliner". It's a versatile unpressurised little nineteen-seater. Developed by de Havilland Canada, the *Otter* can be fitted with floats or skis to deal with the country's lakes and mountains. While not ideal for the Highlands and Islands it is retained by Loganair because of its short field performance and a fixed undercarriage which makes it the only aircraft approved for the beach landing in Barra. Most aircraft have retractable gears which, of course, would expose them to salt and sand on the beach, with consequent corrosion.

Even with a fixed undercarriage the *Twin Otter* is washed down after returning from Barra. Flying usually only once daily to Barra amounts to very little aircraft utilisation, and so to improve the economics, the *Twin Otter* is also used at times on the Campbeltown service (the joke is that it could almost land across the wide runway at Machrihanish!)

Without the "wee plane", anyone in and around Campbeltown needing specialist medical treatment faces a long and twisting road journey of around 130 miles to Glasgow. The little plane is a life saviour, as well as providing tourists access to one of the most beautiful areas of Scotland. An example of what this really means to locals dawned on me when I had occasion to fly to Glasgow for a meeting. In this case the aircraft was a small *Saab*. My brother-in-law who happened to be staying with me in Carradale offered to drop me off at the airport. When we reached Glasgow, after a flight of less than thirty minutes, I called my wife to ask if Ian was home. Not yet was the answer, he's still driving back from Machrihanish! No wonder the Highlands and Islands value the current air services bequeathed to them by the pioneers. By the way, when the Glasgow cabbie asked as I stepped in, "Where are we going?" and I said Barlinnie, he replied with the humour of a true Glaswegian; "Found you out at last!" Maybe I did look a little shifty that morning.

The airport itself borders the world-renowned original Machrihanish golf course founded in 1876 with a layout worked on by Old Tom Morris and J.H. Taylor. The new swanky Machrihanish Dunes links nearby is handy for well-heeled Americans to park their private jets at the air base and stroll over for a round on the course, marketing itself as "golf the way it was". A claim verified by the sheep grazing on it (not to mention the fierce winds off the Atlantic that tests the game of even the best players). The golfers also get a close-up of that "wee plane" which, apart from taking locals to hospital appointments in the big city, is handy for shopping trips and meeting relatives. Surprisingly, as it seems, I could perhaps have seen and heard something a lot more spectacular in the skies above the little fishing harbour of Carradale – the space shuttle. Most people with an interest in aviation know that the main runway in the modern Machrihanish airport is one of the largest in Europe, at 10,000 feet massively more than is needed for normal commercial aviation.

As is often the case, much of the huge spending to create the runway and surrounding facilities was driven by the military. From 1990 to 1995 NATO and the MOD between them spent more than £50 million here – on a relatively unheralded remote spot, on Scotland's west coast. The US authorities showed their appreciation a few years ago when Machrihanish staged a splendid little air show. The huge field was mainly dotted by craft from many of Scotland's thriving aero clubs and well-preserved examples of bi-planes and other early pioneering planes. It was a great day out for the locals. But the highlight was a flyover by the latest US jet bomber, the *B1*, usually hidden away in air bases in England. This plane known as the *Lancer* holds all sorts of records for speed and armament and was used in combat in Iraq. The fact that the Americans took the latest in technology to a little local air show demonstrates a respectful response to friendships made locally. Maybe the fact the USAF top brass in Machrihanish used a hotel just a mile or so away for the airport as an unofficial mess also played a role in the decision to fly north. That little hotel's cocktail bar had, by the way, a collection of malt whisky that would not have looked out of place in a glossy Manhattan hostelry.

Around this time the airport was also a base for a team of US Navy "Seals", a commando group of around twenty people called a Naval Special Warfare Detachment. All this American activity was concentrated on a group of buildings, one designed to hold nuclear weapons. Though official sources suggest none were ever on-site. But that's another story . . .

During this period NASA was also building its space shuttle programme. There was a massive amount of game planning for disaster around the risky journeys into space and to the moon and back. The possibility of what was called "a trans-oceanic abort" of the shuttle led to a search for alternative landing sites. Machrihanish ticked many of the boxes – reasonably far from large centres of population, an open approach from the west particularly, and it already had a US military presence. None of the well-documented space shuttle tragedies involved a landing back on earth. Nonetheless Machrihanish was, according to some, officially certified as an emergency landing site for the shuttle which continued to fly until 2011. Across the world there are many US, or US-controlled, bases with long runways which as well as being capable of providing a landing strip for a shuttle, could make room for a converted 747 to airlift it home.

You wonder what the fliers of the wood and canvas "string-bags" who used the original Argyll airport when it opened in 1918 would have made of the sight of a shuttle sweeping down from space. The original airport in at the back of Westport beach, a favourite surf and sea kayaking spot, was built on an ideal site – open ocean on one side and an uncluttered approach from the east. Visibility was superb – like Prestwick, normally fog free – and the only possible defect was the frequency of strong winds from the west. Fliers and golfers must take it into account, though for the surfers it is a blessing, pushing the huge rollers that have built up on the open Atlantic, on to a long flat smooth sand beach. Locals and visitors alike enjoy strolling beside the sea and taking pleasure in the thought that if you looked out over the breakers and had the eyesight of Superman, the first land you would see would be the east coast of the United States.

This "proximity" to the other side of the pond was also important as it featured in early transatlantic radio experiments. A huge steel mast was erected at Machrihanish to link Scotland to a similar tower in eastern Canada. Sadly, this construction, which had it been preserved would have made a good tourist attraction, was left to rot. Nothing to see of it now. A shame. The Canadians, however, made several similar sites around Nova Scotia dedicated historic monuments, one listed as far back as 1939. It is a splendid example of turning history into commercial success and providing recreational and educational space for families. If you are ever in the area, give these sites a visit to see the chance we in Scotland failed to take. Signal Hill in Newfoundland is perhaps the best, a tribute to Marconi's genius which helped transform the world. Scotland's connections to these experiments are largely forgotten. Sometimes we are o'er modest in assessing our achievements.

The flying base itself, a few miles outside Campbeltown, was originally called Machrihanish Aerodrome and Mooring Out Station. The "mooring out" referred to the ability to service airships. Machrihanish was a subsidiary station to a more regularly used airship base at Luce Bay, fifty miles south down the coast. Used by the Royal Naval Air Service it was more suitable for mooring such craft: as well as the winds at Machrihanish there was a lack of woodland in the area, which made the "gasbags" even more vulnerable. Though airships were ideal for surveillance of the Western Approaches in time of war, it seems not all that many used Machrihanish. One airship used by the Royal Naval Air Service at the time was the *Sea Scout*, much smaller than the *Zeppelins* at around 112 feet long and slow at fifty mph with a three-man crew. Its main attraction was that it could remain airborne for ten hours or so.

With military disregard of superstition, the field officially became under the control of the newly formed RAF on April 1, 1918. This heralded a busy few months before the end of the war and eighteen *DH6s* were deployed on anti-submarine patrols over the Firth of Clyde. This de Havilland was an interesting aircraft and more than 2,000 were built for the use of the Navy and the Army's Royal Flying Corps. It is claimed that it could fly safely at the astonishingly low speed of thirty mph and was ideal for searching for U-boat periscope trails, as well as an easy to fly all-rounder that made it ideal for training. At the end of the First World War, the field began to be used for civilian flights to Islay and Renfrew, which served Glasgow. The service was run by Midland and Scottish Air Ferries, which operated the country's first passenger internal air between Campbeltown and Glasgow in April 1933 using a de Havilland *Fox*. That history-making flight carried Glasgow newspapers to the "wee town". The newspaper delivery business became a major revenue maker for many of the pioneering airlines who also worked as air ambulances and with the Post Office.

Midland & Scottish was one of the pioneering predecessors of the old Scottish Airways It was founded by entrepreneur John Sword who with his wife Christine put up the seed capital of £20,000. It is remarkable that even as far back as the thirties the list of towns and islands served by air included Tiree, South Uist, Inverness, North Uist, Campbeltown, Barra, Perth and Skye. Along with these standalone early airlines there was the Railway Air Service (a rather odd choice of name, as few railways ever took to the air!) which was an attempt by railway companies to beat off competitors in the travel game.

This was at the start of the new era of international air travel. The first international arrival at Renfrew, near Glasgow, for example, was in 1936 when a German international football team landed to take on Scotland. The incoming *Junkers* flaunted that sinister symbol, a swastika. The result was a draw but that old chant from Scottish terraces when we play Germany, "Who won the war?", was not heard. (Though I did hear it at Hampden Park Stadium in Glasgow, on a spring night in 1960 at one of the greatest matches ever played: Real Madrid v Eintracht Frankfurt, which ended with the Germans "beaten out of the park", as a Glaswegian would say. We have long memories . . .) With the arrival of the Second World War in 1939 the original Kintyre runways and facilities were not up to the job. In 1941 the airfield was requisitioned by the Fleet Air Arm and became HMS Landrail. A new runway to the north-west of the original was built in jig-time and opened in June as the Royal Naval Air Station Strabane. It very quickly became RNAS Machrihanish, with the old airport becoming HMS Landrail II. In the war it was a busy place with pilot training, anti-submarine patrols and acting as a base for convoy escort duty. The once quiet lands of this remote spot at the end of the Kintyre Peninsula echoed to take-offs and landings galore and the locals were treated to close-ups of the most modern of weapons. Early arrivals were the iconic *Fairy Swordfish* and other aircraft using the base included *Spitfires* for pilot training and *Bristol Beaufighters*. On occasion an aircraft carrier would cruise offshore and pilots were able to practise the tricky art of landing on a pitching deck, sometimes in darkness. The archives contain claims that Machrihanish at one time was one of the three busiest air bases in Britain. But the air quietened with the end of hostilities. The old runways were returned to agriculture and the modern base eventually placed on care and maintenance. But there were exciting times ahead.

The shuttle was not the only connection Machrihanish has with the space race. That impressive runway was also used for the testing of top-secret US stealth aircraft. And, if you are among the gullible, who believe every speculation in the tabloids, you might also believe that aliens are kept in a secret hangar guarded night and day by armed soldiers. I want to put on record that I do not believe a word of it and the only alien suspects in the area are a tiny number of low-lifers from Campbeltown or Tarbert who may have overindulged in mind-bending drugs. Nor do I give any credence to reports that the skies above Bonnybridge, not all that far away in the Central Belt, are a sort of Scottish space Bermuda Triangle – despite those regular reports in the tabloids who find such controversies are ideal for stimulating sales in quiet days. It has even been claimed that the town of Bonnybridge itself, near Falkirk, has become the UFO capital of the world with more than 300 sightings of Unidentified Flying Objects reported every year. Hang on guys – ever thought that the strange objects in the sky might just be reflections in the clouds of gas flares being burned off from the nearby oil refinery at Grangemouth? Mind you, the idea of such an unlikely wee town being at the centre of alien activity is more fun. That Machrihanish is a holding base for little green men is just about as fantastic. However, the notion that the area swarms with armed guards keeping watch on ET just might have come about as a result of the fact that one hangar was purpose-built to contain nuclear weapons and was therefore unlikely to have open doors for anyone who stumbled past. Though there is no official record of nukes being stored at the base. All the facilities and the long runway (by the way it's not all that long nowadays; even Shannon, a quick flip across the Irish Sea is in fact longer) might have fuelled the flames of controversy.

If, in a humourless and unimaginative way, you dismiss the wild theories of Machrihanish as a kind of Scottish Roswell, or Area 51 in Nevada, it must be said, it is a pretty quiet spot today. Military activity declined sharply from the 1990s, particularly when the US Navy handed back control to the MOD in 1995. These days the daily flights to Glasgow are about the only aircraft movements. The Army still has occasional training sorties to the area and you might see an odd *Lockheed Hercules* dropping in, or some youngsters from the Air Training Corps on exercise. But for excitement in this beautiful part of Scotland you would be better to try surfing, sea kayaking or taking on the world-famous golf courses. Still there is no denying that Kintyre played a major role in pioneering air travel and in both World Wars was vital to the defence of Britain. It has not the fame of airports like Prestwick, Glasgow or Edinburgh. Maybe it should.

8

From Lanarkshire to the Top of the World

There are many candidates for a place on the leaderboard in any search for the title of "greatest" pilot ever. It is not possible to be definitive – you are comparing different men flying different machines in different eras. But two Scots were for a time at least literally on top of the world – the pilots of the two biplanes that were the first machines to fly over Everest. One was Douglas Douglas-Hamilton (Lord Clydesdale), the other Flight Lieutenant David McIntyre. Clydesdale led the team that conquered Everest (more than 29,000 ft.) in April 1933 to look down on the highest point on earth. It was a magnificent achievement, long in the planning. The great peak has always challenged mountaineers and has taken many lives. It also attracted early aviators. One of the great names in early flying was Englishman Sir Alan Cobham whose exploits included the first flights from London to Cape Town and back. Nine years before the successful Scottish flight, Cobham made an attempt that now seems bold to the point of foolishness.

Without oxygen he managed to ascend to only around 15,000 feet – about half the altitude he needed to achieve. It was a rare failure in a career marked with spectacular success, including flying to Australia and back to a landing on the Thames near the Houses of Parliament.

It seems apt that Westminster was where the plot for a successful attempt on Everest was developed. One day John Buchan, author of *The Thirty-Nine Steps* among other novels, met Lord Clydesdale in the Commons. The man who was to lead the team that conquered Everest was something of a polymath. At the time he was talking to Buchan he was the second youngest Member of Parliament and a former Scottish Amateur Middleweight Boxing Champion. In addition, he was already an experienced pilot. He had commanded the 602 (City of Glasgow) of the Auxiliary Air Force. In their conversation Buchan informed his young friend that more than Cobham had tried to fly over the world's highest peak. Two Americans, Richard Halliburton and Meyro Stevens had made the attempt, but like Cobham were unable to get higher than halfway to the height needed. Buchan also intimated that there were rumours that the French and Germans were working on aircraft to achieve the feat. The race was on. The great writer believed a first flight over Everest would establish Britain as a world leader in the developing world of aviation. In Buchan's mind an expedition would provide air survey information of great importance, as well as dent the growing reputation of the United States as the pre-eminent nation in the rush to develop air travel. The trip would require the most advanced aircraft of the time and technology to defeat the oxygen problem that had so far defied attempts at the feat. He also realised that photography would be a vital part of the expedition's task.

The young Lanarkshire aristocrat quickly grasped that Buchan was making a lot of sense. He knew, too, that despite the demands it would place on the mechanical side it would also take the courage of the aircrews themselves to successfully complete the flights. How ambitious the whole project was is demonstrated by the fact that at that time aircraft were not pressurised and the use of oxygen masks was in early development. Flying in the icy temperatures required to conquer the highest peak in the world had never been done. Committee meetings were many, but even examined in the comfort of a London club, brandy or port in hand in front of a roaring fire, there was no escape from the dangers and difficulty of what was being planned. But Lord Clydesdale was as they say these days "up for it".

The politics of it made the idea even more suitable. This was in the time of the National Government and India's fate was already a concern. A success on Everest would bring world attention to India and British rule. An extra attraction to Clydesdale was that the adventure could add to scientific development. Another bonus was it that would allow him to visit the troubled continent at first hand, something that appealed. So, he swiftly accepted an invitation to join the 1932 British Flight to the Mount Everest Committee. Also on this body was Colonel Stewart Blacker, who was the first to suggest such a flight, although as far back as 1918 the notion that this would be a good flight was proposed by a mountaineer with an interest in physiology and high altitudes yet was not acted on. This was an interesting twist of fate – Blacker's grandfather Valentine was the first Surveyor-General of India and had been responsible for the mapping of Hindustan. Colonel Valentine was apparently a volatile sort of man who got himself in a duel that killed his opponent as well as himself. Strangely one of his successors in the post of Surveyor-General was none other than Sir George Everest. The signs looked good.

Stewart Blacker himself was a remarkable character. He learned to fly as early as 1911 and fought in the trenches of the First World War (whilst being injured by German machine gunfire) before transferring to the Royal Flying Corps in 1915. Much decorated, he had also been involved in military operations in Persia and had a deep knowledge of India and Central Asia. He was also something of an inventor. Though one of his forays into this field did not yield significant success. From the first days of "dogfighting" in the air a major problem was finding a way to firing a machine gun at an opponent directly in your sights without damaging your own propeller. Something that was eventually solved by synchronisation of the machine gun and the revolutions of the propeller. Blacker tried out his own solution on a specially adapted plane but the bullets managed to hit his own propeller, in effect shooting himself down. He survived the crash though he sustained severe back injuries. When he recovered, he transferred back to the Army.

In 1932 the Everest committee had an HQ in Chelsea in London and Blacker made the following proposals seeking the approval of the Royal Geographical Society:

1. To reconnoitre and to map by air photographic survey the almost unknown southern slopes of the massif of Mount Everest, thereby making an important contribution to geography and to its allied sciences.
2. To produce a cinematograph film of exceptional attraction and real worth, not only to science, to the world and education in general, and to combine with this the creation of a new height record for an aeroplane, carrying two persons, thereby adding value to both achievements.
3. To carry out these feats with purely British personnel and thereby give a stimulus to enterprise.

The Geographical Society backed the proposal and wrote to the Secretary of State for India expressing confidence that the flight would produce valuable scientific results. The Air Ministry was also in on the act and most importantly so was the RAF School of Photography at Farnborough. The whole idea gained much support. A leading article in *The Scotsman*, some weeks before the flight, slightly pompously summed up the hope of the public: "Success will mean a triumph of British grit and also British materials, besides resulting in an extension of human knowledge of the planet which we inhabit." There was a notion, too, that the flight might help throw light on the fate of George Mallory and Andrew Irvine, who disappeared on an attempt to climb Everest in 1929. (In any event this, not surprisingly, didn't shine any light on what had happened many years before. The howling winds, fierce temperature of fifty below saw to that. A rapid visual search from the cockpits of the planes looking down at the "roof of the world" below showed no sign of bodies or climbing gear).

The four men who carried out the successful flight on April 19, 1933, were an interesting mix: Lord Clydesdale (RAF squadron leader Douglas Douglas-Hamilton) was the leader and in his plane with him was the intrepid Stewart Blacker. The following plane was piloted by the legendary Flight Lieutenant David McIntyre. Both were young adventurers – Douglas-Hamilton was thirty and McIntyre twenty-eight! McIntyre, who was to go on to make a great mark on aviation in Scotland, had as his colleague, a cinematographer from Gaumont British News, Sidney Bonnett, whose shots were spectacularly successful and helped publicise an adventure taking place thousands of miles from Britain. Without him the true value of the expedition, and the risks the fliers took, would never have created the worldwide interest in the feat. It was gold-star public relations to have him on the plane with McIntyre.

The film shot by cameraman Bonnett was the basis of a remarkable short film that in 1936 won an Oscar in the documentary section. You can watch *Wings over Everest* on YouTube. Scratchy film, poor quality sound, but plenty of stiff upper lip. The film mixed real-life footage of the flight with a scripted telling of the adventure that featured the real people involved, not actors. The sensational views of the Himalayas as seen from the planes was an aid to climbers Edmund Hillary and Tenzing Norgay, who studied the terrain as seen from the air in 1953 before becoming the first men to reach the top of the world on foot. Watching the film today, you realise that the fact that both Douglas-Hamilton and McIntyre had the good looks and style of the Hollywood actors of the day must have helped to win that prized and well-deserved Oscar. Part actuality, part recreation, it is one of the finest insights into what early aviation was like that you will ever see.

Away from the cameras the reality and scale of what was proposed soon highlighted the usual problem of such expeditions – it was going to cost a massive amount of money. This was discovered in a way that also had a touch of a Hollywood script about it. The money to fund the expedition came from a former London chorus girl who was the daughter of a Lambeth draper and whose original name was Fanny Radmall. Quite a girl, Fanny had a succession of rich husbands after first eloping at the tender age of sixteen with an heir to the Bass Brewery fortune. When she died, she was Lady Houston and a millionaire. She was obviously a looker but in addition she was bright, generous and very interested in early aviation. And you could say she played a major role in the United Kingdom winning the Battle of Britain early in the Second World War. Lucy, as she was now known, had bankrolled the British entry into the Schneider Air Trophy speed races. The work done to create the beautiful fast and agile British entry led directly to the design of the *Spitfire* that was so successful for the RAF. She was an obvious target for the fundraisers. It is said that when Douglas-Hamilton first approached her, she was reluctant to give him the money, in order to stop him "committing suicide on Everest". But apparently the pilot who was to lead the expedition said it was as safe as walking round Hampstead Heath on a foggy night! A Wodehousian remark, though far from the truth, that charmed the lady, who promptly signed a massive cheque, funding the Houston Mount Everest Flying Expedition.

Securing financial backing accomplished, attention was concentrated on the aircraft to be used. The chosen craft were a *Westland PV-3* and a *Westland PV-6*, both single engine biplanes. They had been modified for the flight, particularly the *PV-3* which was piloted by Douglas-Hamilton. Whilst neither craft was pressurised, both had oxygen fed from bottles to the aviators. The flyers wore special gloves and thick cumbersome heated clothing and goggles. (Film of the crews waddling in this awkward clothing towards the cockpits of the flimsy planes looked for the entire world very similar to that of the astronauts of a different era, boarding spacecraft in their flight suits with life support machines in hand). The specially prepared planes were disassembled and sent by sea in packing cases to India then reassembled. When ready they were ferried to Purnea, the sight of a primitive, but large and safe, grass airfield on a great plain adjacent to the foothills of the Himalayas. An early attempt to fly over Everest was abandoned because of hazy conditions and the planes were returned to base. But on the morning of April 3, 1933, a light aircraft returned from a "recce" to report that conditions were probably as good as you would get. The order was given to "Go!", but the flight was not without moments of drama. Hampstead Heath on a foggy night suddenly seemed preferable to the situation the aviators were in. The swirling winds round the mountain peaks created difficult flying conditions and at one stage threatened to push the flimsy biplanes downwards rather than help them stagger the last few thousand feet to get over the summit. But at the last moment a sudden updraft helped the toiling craft to their ideal height. The oxygen system also gave trouble to both Douglas-Hamilton and cameraman Bonnett and at one stage they were in danger of passing out, but somehow they managed to stay awake. The engines were functioning well and as height was lost they returned to the dusty flatness of Purnea. All was well. The sense of relief as wheels touched grass must have been great. It was over. Job done; history made. And plans to glide back to solid ground more than fifty miles away had the fuel or engines given trouble at around 30,000 feet were just a memory.

9

Death of a Legend and a
Base called Slaughter Hall

Aviation in Scotland in the years after the Second World War enjoyed a legacy of the great conflict – the collection of military air stations that were to be found abandoned, or little used, in many parts of the countryside. Some like RNAS Abbotsinch, a couple of miles or so from Glasgow's previous main airport at Renfrew, eventually became hubs of civil aviation. And for a time, East Fortune handled Edinburgh's commercial air traffic. Other stations slipped into decay though the actual runways, built to last, were a godsend to weekend fliers and private aviation. The wartime brick buildings deteriorated and often appeared as crumbling ruins glimpsed from the nearest road, giving little hint to the visitor of the days when air traffic controllers, weather forecasters, mechanics, Women's Auxiliary Air Force personnel and pilots lived there. Charterhall in the Borders, one such place, could cope with almost 2,000 service men and women.

The opportunity of using long stretches of tarmac was not missed by the motor racing fraternity. All you needed was a supply of straw bales and you could map out a track as testing as you like. I can remember as a boy being taken by my dad to both Charterhall in the Borders and Turnberry in Ayrshire to watch well-attended race meetings. At Turnberry I got an early warning that, as it said on the ticket: "motor racing is dangerous". One competitor, with no seat harness, was tipped out of his tumbling car onto the grass a few yards from spectators. Fortunately, he was unhurt and soon on his feet walking back to the paddock. Another racer, the legendary Jack Brabham was spotted in action at Charterhall where he arrived by road, towing his race car behind his road car. No private jets or huge motor homes to entertain the insiders in these days. Others who raced here included Stirling Moss, Giuseppe Farina and, of course, the Borderer Jim Clark who saw his first race here. The racing team Ecurie Ecosse used the track as a testing ground for many years.

But Charterhall has a special place in flying history too. Richard Hillary, one of the most noted Battle of Britain aces and author of the much lauded *The Last Enemy*, lost his life, along with his observer Wilfred Fison, near the station in a night-flying exercise when their *Bristol Blenheim* crashed in January 1943. They had only been in the air a few minutes when they came down near a farm. Hillary, Fison and other aircrew from the station who died in the Second World War are remembered in a plaque unveiled in 2001. They were many and indeed the airfield was nicknamed "Slaughter Hall" since so many trainee pilots had accidents. In one month early in the forties there were seven major crashes. Hillary had joined Oxford University Air Squadron and the Royal Air Force Voluntary Reserve in 1939. He was the son of a high-ranking Australian government official and had been sent to Britain to be educated. A descendant of the founder of the Royal National Lifeboat Institution, his first posting after training to fly *Spitfires* was to RAF Montrose. Sent back south he soon showed his ability in air-to-air combat and in one week in the Battle of Britain it was claimed he had officially shot down five *ME109*s with two more probably destroyed and one damaged. Adept in combat, he was also masterly with pen and ink. In *The Last Enemy* he described the *Spitfires*, an aircraft he loved, as having: "the clear-cut beauty, the wicked simplicity of their lines."

Still, it was a dangerous love affair. Hillary became one of the most famous of the "guinea pigs" treated by the legendary plastic surgeon Archibald McIndoe in his hospital at East Grinstead in Sussex. The flying ace had himself been shot down by a *109* and was trapped in his burning cockpit before managing to parachute into the Channel and be rescued by the Margate lifeboat. He endured months of painful surgery to his badly burned face and hands before he got back into the pilot's seat. His account of his treatment and recovery is heart-rending and uplifting. Despite being barely able to handle a knife and fork with his mangled hands he managed to talk his way back into the air. When he died in the Charterhall crash he was on a conversion course from fighters to become a light bomber pilot. His ashes were poignantly scattered over the English Channel, scene of many of his dogfights in his beloved "Spit".

The Borders station was mostly a training base and at times an outpost of RAF fighter command and served from its opening in 1940 till the end of the war. But it also played a role in the First World War for the Royal Flying Corps and such famous aircraft as the de Havilland *DH6* and the *Avro 504K* were regularly seen in the area. During the thirties it had returned to agriculture. The story of Turnberry airfield on the other side of the country, in Ayrshire, has many similarities to that of Charterhall. It had been used as a training base in the closing years of the

First World War by the Royal Flying Corps, but the land was returned to agriculture and golf in the thirties before reconstruction of a much larger military aerodrome in 1941. Presumably the flat land at the edge of the sea and the fog-free reputation of the area, like Prestwick a few miles up the coast road to Glasgow, were reasons for the choice of the site. In its RFC heyday it was No 1 School of Aerial Fighting before being merged with a "school of aerial gunnery" that had been based at Loch Doon a few miles inland, becoming No 1 Fighting School (North West Area) in the spring of 1918. The student pilots had to be quick learners as the courses lasted a mere three weeks. Though, of course, the flying machines in those days were a tad less complicated than supersonic jets. During the Second World War the famous railway hotel was used as a Navy hospital and it is said that as many as 200 died there from their injuries. Between the wars the hotel's two famous golf courses, the *Ailsa* and the *Arran*, were rebuilt. Today's golfers can pause to have a look at a monument on a rise overlooking the twelfth green of the *Ailsa* course, honouring the memory of airmen who died.

In the Second World War, apart from training, *Liberator* aircraft used the base for anti-submarine patrols out over the nearby Atlantic. Interestingly the famous Barnes Wallis bouncing bombs of the Dambusters of 618 Squadron were tested by planes flying out of Turnberry. Like Charterhall, Turnberry was, for the second time, turned back to farming and golf. And again, like Charterhall, its runways were used as a motor racing circuit. Its proximity to Glasgow and the abundance of tourist accommodation and attractions in the area allowed it, for a time, to attract large crowds. One of the most memorable events was the *Daily Record* Race Meeting in 1952. Although the track as laid out was featureless and flat, with none of the amenities of a modern Grand Prix, the racing was good and both Charterhall and

Turnberry were able to pay prize money that could attract the very best drivers and teams from down south. The main event was won by Reg Parnell driving a *BRM* followed by teammate Ken Wharton with one of Scotland's most famous drivers, Ron Flockhart, third in an *ERA*. Mike Hawthorn took the pole in a *Thinwall Special*. A quality field of highfliers indeed.

10

Ferry Across the Pond . . . and the Beauty of Concorde

My own most vivid memory of Prestwick airport is of *Concorde* making a low-level demonstration flight over the Ayrshire town. A sunny day, blue sky, and a close-up view of what, to my mind, remains the most beautiful aircraft ever built, is unforgettable. The brilliant white livery, unusual delta shape wing, and the ear-splitting roar of the engines brought gasps from the thousands who watched it bank spectacularly out over the sea and make a majestic turn back inland for an earth-shaking run a few feet above that famous long runway. No matter that it was built to thunder across the Atlantic, filled with the wealthy elite of America and Britain, it still thrilled folk who would never get the chance to squeeze into the narrow cabin and sip champagne, nibbling the best of steaks while travelling as they used to say, "faster than a speeding bullet".

An older memory was a bit of battered and burned aluminium scraped out of the sands near the end of the main runway during a Second World War holiday on the Ayrshire coast. It went home as a souvenir. But I was too young to really grasp its significance. That piece of crumpled and fire-stained metal had come from the burned-out shell of a wartime US plane, part of a huge Second World War air ferry operation, that had crashed near the airport. The transatlantic air ferry played a major role in the Allied victory. Hundreds of war planes manufactured in the US were flown "across the pond" to Prestwick and delivered onward to European bases. But a high price was paid in the form of fatal crashes in and around the airport. In an interview, Scott Grier, of Loganair fame, told me:

> Talking of the air ferry reminded me of a lunch in 1992 I attended at Prestwick to mark the fiftieth anniversary of the Lend Lease Programme. I particularly remember one of the celebrated ferry pilots was Miss Lettice Curtis. In her fantastic speech she told us they had to study winds and navigated across the Atlantic by reference to the stars. Made a great impression on me. Never ceases to amaze me that such was the speed of technological advance thereafter, that only twenty-seven years later there was a man on the moon.

The view from Prestwick out over the Firth of Clyde, a holiday playground in peacetime, is dominated by the mountainous barrier of the island of Arran. Prestwick, as noted, has an impressive long runway and a record of having good visibility when other airports were closed. These days it is a perfect site for heavy, powerful jets. But in its early days those mountains threatened underpowered craft taking off and heading west. My souvenir came from a plane that had barely got beyond the beach before it crashed. Many others did stagger the few miles across the Firth of Clyde only to fail to clear the top of Goatfell, or one of the other high peaks on the island known as "Scotland in miniature". Researchers in recent years have uncovered several crash sites on the island. But for planes flying out of Prestwick there was another danger not as well known – the Kintyre Peninsula.

In a remarkably detailed book *Deadly Peninsula*, two researchers, David W. Earl and Peter Dobson, say that more than fifty aircraft came to grief in the thirty-mile length of this part of Scotland known as "the mainland" island because only a strip of land a couple of miles or so, between Tarbert and West Loch Tarbert, prevent Kintyre being a true island. (A fact exploited by invading Vikings, who in the time of Magnus Barefoot, a Norse king (1073–1103), are said to have claimed authority over any part of Scotland they could "sail" around and dragged their longships across the portage between the east and west lochs. An intriguing story and, true or not, there is plenty of evidence of the Norse invaders in the hills and glens of this beautiful, but dangerous, part of the world). As a regular commuter between Glasgow and Campbeltown for many years I got to know north Kintyre well and a welcome stop on my drive to Carradale was a quick pint at the pleasant West Loch Hotel. There, midges permitting, you could sit outside and enjoy the scenery. An old wooden fishing boat rotting on rocks just across from the hotel added a quaint touch to the scenery. But there was another unseen wreck nearby. In the waters just offshore in the summer of 1943, four crew members and sixteen passengers died when a *Fokker 22* of Coastal Command crashed after an in-flight fire en route from Tiree to the RAF field at Abbotsinch (later to become Glasgow Airport).

Tiree has an interesting place in the history of flying in the Western Isles. As far back as 1929 the potential of a strip of flat land known as "The Reef" was spotted. Midland & Scottish Airways among others used a grass strip there in the 1930s. In the early days of the Second World War the Ministry of War requisitioned the land and began building a proper airfield with labour imported from Ireland and even some workers from Glasgow's jails, tough men suitable for hard toil. The field is in use today and is vital to tourism in the islands. During the war it had been exceptionally busy with fighters seeking out U-boats on the Western Approaches, meteorological work and air sea rescue. There was another fatal accident in 1944 when two *Halifax* planes collided in low cloud near the landing strip. One of those killed in this incident was the grandson of the then Czech diplomat, Jan Masaryk.

On the mainland one of the most notable fatal crashes was of a *Liberator*, part of the Atlantic Ferry operation that is such a significant part of the history of Prestwick airport, which crashed near Campbeltown in the summer of 1941.The *Liberator* was a heavy four-engined bomber. But because it did not have self-sealing fuel tanks, the RAF decided that it was unsuitable for combat and, with guns removed, suitable seating installed and a passenger oxygen supply fitted, it was valuable to Ferry Command as transatlantic transport. This particular fatal flight had originated in Montreal and was heading for Scotland. At the time Prestwick was being enlarged and developed so the *Liberator* was detailed to land at a nearby strip at Heathfield. The pilot, an experienced transatlantic flier, was a bit unhappy about the conditions on approach and decided to divert to Squires Gate, near Blackpool, but as was not unusual in the war, there was a communications problem and confusion about the weather reports. It turned out the English aerodrome was fogged in. The last messages indicated that the ferry plane was heading back to the Prestwick area in difficult conditions, but the airwaves went ominously silent and the *Liberator* flew into a hill a few miles from Campbeltown. All eleven on board, crew and passengers, died. As was normal on such ferry flights, those who lost their lives were a mixture of civilian, military and diplomatic personnel. One passenger was Captain Sherwood Picking of the US Navy who in 1925 had captained *V–1*, the largest US submarine of the time. During the Second World War he was a Navy attaché in Washington and was on his way to meetings in London. Another who perished was Count Guy Comte de Baillet-Latour, the son of Count Henri who was President of the International Olympic Committee of the time. Guy was working out of the Belgium Embassy in London. Some aircraft parts were still on the hill in 2017, but a memorial plaque was not to be found. Many of the other planes that were caught out by the deadly peninsula were much smaller than the *Liberator* and often were on training exercises. But looking back on the toll of lives taken by this small and remote part of Scotland is a poignant reminder of the price paid by aviators and their passengers in the Second World War.

It is somewhat ironic that two of the best documented major disasters at Prestwick happened on low-level approaches and the mountains played no part in either tragedy. After the Second World War, and before the jet age, Prestwick, Shannon in Ireland and Gander in Newfoundland were vital refuelling stops for the new breed of luxury piston engine airliners. Passenger traffic across the Atlantic was growing fast in this new peacetime world. But planes such as the *Lockheed Constellation* – a contender for one of the most beautiful of propeller driven giants – and the *Boeing Stratocruiser* had limited range and few of the sophisticated navigation aids of a modern jet. The *Lockheed* aircraft, incidentally, was notable apart from its beauty for its three abreast tail fins, a most unusual configuration, and the height it stood above the runway when parked. The designers realised that the plane they were creating would benefit from an extra-tall tail plane, but if the optimum size was built the "Connie" would not fit into the aircraft hangars of the time. So, the three tail planes plan was put into place though it would be more complex and less efficient. The issue of the height of the body of the plane above the runway was dictated by a technical issue – the propellers were designed to be longer than the norm, hence the extra-long legs of the undercarriage. All this did little to affect the beauty of the design. At the Melbourne Air Show a few years ago I saw one of the few remaining "Connies" on display. Like the *Concorde* or *Comet*, it demonstrated the adage about planes – "if it looks right it flies right".

The "Connie" I saw that day in Australia was highly polished, its bare metal fuselage sparkling in the antipodean sunlight, different weather conditions indeed from those endured by the workhorse *KLM* liner (call sign PH–TEN) that crashed at Prestwick in 1948. On a wild October night, that KLM "Connie" named *Nijmegen* suffered what the accident inquiry later prosaically called a "controlled flight into terrain" on a stopover before a trip to America. All on board – ten crew and thirty passengers – died. The plane was under the control of a man considered to be a great pilot of the era, Koene Dirk Parmentier. A vastly experienced flier, he was the airline's chief pilot and the winner of a prestigious pre-war air race. The doomed flight left Amsterdam, scheduled to stop at Prestwick or, if the weather was difficult there, to go on to Shannon. From Prestwick the intention was to stop with cargo in Iceland. The Dutch weather forecasters told the skipper that the weather at Prestwick was slight cloud, but that it was likely to dissipate by the time the "Connie" reached Scotland. This was more than seventy years ago, and forecasters did not have the benefit of satellite information and many of the modern aids to predicting weather accurately. Tragically this forecast was almost completely wrong.

When the KLM plane neared Prestwick the weather, already bad, was deteriorating and it was even worse at Shannon. All accidents to some extent are a combination of circumstance. This was a classic case of a series of different types of errors leading to a major disaster. In Holland the departure of *Nijmegen* had been delayed by loading the cargo for Iceland. This had meant that Parmentier had not picked up a forecast from Prestwick telling him how bad the weather really was. He was also not aware that earlier that night two SAS planes had aborted plans to land at Prestwick because of weather. He headed on, but because of crosswinds swithered whether to use Prestwick's main runway or an alternate that would allow him to head into the wind. This shorter runway had no radar approach system. Another piece in the jigsaw of disaster was that a Morse message to the plane from Prestwick was missed because the crew had switched to voice control as it approached the airfield in stormy darkness. Had they got the message telling of a change in the weather, a landing on the main runway might have been seen easier? Inexplicably there was another complication – the charts the KLM chief pilot was using were seriously inaccurate. Information on high ground nearby and the height of pylons carrying the huge power load (132,000 volts) of the main national grid to the south of Scotland were both wrong. In the dark, and in the clouds, Parmentier opted for the alternate runway – a decision not criticised by the inquiry – and as he neared the airport manoeuvring to line up with the runway he hit the electricity cables. Now on fire the "Connie" attempted to head for an emergency landing but hit the ground five miles short of the airport. But the agony of this catalogue of errors was not over. Emergency services did not reach the crash site for ninety minutes because of confusion as to who was responsible to go to the site. Six people survived the initial crash, but all died within twenty-four hours.

This is the story of what can bring that disturbing phrase "controlled flight into terrain" into play. Many factors were involved but perhaps the most significant of all is an error the court of inquiry called astonishing. The charts the crew relied on had been copied from war-era US Airforce charts. The inquiry said: "KLM has relied on maps from a foreign authority when detailed and correct maps were available from the Ordnance Survey, the UK's national authority." Astonishing is an understatement.

Human error also featured in a crash six years later when a *Boeing Stratocruiser* of British Overseas Airways (G–ALSA, named "Cathay") hit the ground short of the runway, overturning and bursting into flames. Again, a combination of circumstances led to the disaster. The flight was intended to fly from Heathrow to New York with stopovers at Manchester and Prestwick. Bad weather caused a decision to go direct to Prestwick. The aircraft that was to make the flight was delayed waiting for a late passenger to board and it took off at around twenty to ten in the evening but returned to Heathrow with a mechanical problem an hour and ten minutes later. A new aircraft was substituted, and it left at five minutes after one on Christmas day. Only four of the twenty-five passengers on board were booked for the onward leg to New York and the others were no doubt looking forward to an enjoyable holiday break in Scotland. The crew was also to stay on this side of the Atlantic and a relief crew waited at Prestwick ready to take the *Stratocruiser* to the States. At three thirty in the morning the plane arrived in driving rain and landed just short of the runway killing twenty-eight of the thirty-six people on board including ten women and two children. Seven of the eight survivors were crew members. The inquiry months later declared the cause to be "pilot error". More on that later.

This was a huge Christmas disaster which shocked Scotland and cast a pall over the whole country. It was a human story that filled the papers for days. Christmas 1954 was a sad one. Personal tragedies apart, this crash had an unusual twist. The airliner was far from full for the intended transatlantic crossing. But the 250 mailbags packed into the hold contained a consignment of almost a million pounds worth of uncut diamonds heading for a New York address. A police guard was placed on the crash site and diamonds were still being found a week later. Eventually it was reported that of the forty parcels of diamonds only ninety per cent were recovered. Interestingly the *Constellation* in the previous 1948 crash also had diamonds on board – a much smaller treasure, this time worth only a few thousand pounds worth.

The inquiry into the crash itself investigated possible mechanical failure of some sort involving an air brake, but in the end reported that "the accident was not caused or contributed to by a defect in the plane." The conclusion, it was caused by an error of judgement by the pilot. His mistake was contributed to by the first officer not turning on the landing lights. A factor in these errors could also have been because of problems with the ground landing lights. This verdict seems to me a bit tough on the pilot who was well over his hours thanks to the delay and under rules in place today would not have been allowed to take off from Heathrow.

Flying at Prestwick began as long ago as 1934 (though it was not officially an airport till February 1936) when the large flat area at the back of the town was identified as an ideal spot for a training airfield. Then, as now, the fact that winds blowing in from the Atlantic meant that the area was generally fog-free when further up the Firth, airports adjacent to heavy industry could be closed frequently. (It is often claimed that Prestwick is Britain's only fog-free airport. And certainly, in winters it handles many flights diverted from less fortunate airports. This was particularly true in the occasional really severe winters like those endured in 2009, 2010 and 2011 when large numbers of international flights to Heathrow had to be diverted to Scotland.) By the end of 1935 there were offices, a primitive control tower and the first of many hangars to come on-site. The owner was that dominant figure in early aviation in Scotland – David McIntyre – who had, with the Duke of Hamilton, been the first pilots to fly over Everest in 1933, an adventure discussed earlier. McIntyre, with the Duke's backing, also owned Scottish Aviation Limited. This company went on to manufacture aircraft from 1947 to 1998 in a factory using the old terminal building and some of the early hangars. Three of the most successful craft were the *Prestwick Pioneer* series, the *Bulldog* and the *Jetstream* series. Ironically David McIntyre died in 1957 when on a sales tour and his *Twin Pioneer* suffered a structural failure.

At the start of this chapter two major tragedies were recalled. On a more positive note, the main triumph of the airport, and Scottish Aviation I think, is the success of the *Pioneer*. The protype first flew in 1955 and was featured in that year's Farnborough Air Show. From the start it showed astonishing ability in its short take-off and landing (STOL) capacity and sold well in military and civilian versions. The RAF ordered almost forty aircraft. Other air forces who bought it included the Royal Malaysian Air Force and it became a familiar sight anywhere in the world where the ability to operate from small unsophisticated airfields or just fields mattered. It was particularly suitable for air survey work for map-makers and oil companies. The *Pioneer*'s rugged ability to take off and land almost anywhere did lead to overconfidence in pilots trying to set down on boggy ground or rock-strewn strips and caused the loss of some planes. But overall it became something of an aviation legend.

At the airport itself, full passenger facilities were in place from 1938 and over the years many extensions took the length of the main runway up to an impressive almost 10,000 feet, suitable for the biggest of today's jets. This meant the loss of a unique, but undesirable, feature. Before the final extensions were completed cars, lorries and buses heading into Prestwick from the Glasgow conurbation had to drive at ninety degrees across the main runway. This traffic was controlled by a railway style level crossing system. Not the best solution to the problem (what happened was to move the main roadway round the end of a lengthened runway) but certainly a treat for motorists who patiently waited as the planes shot past feet away from the queuing cars. It was such fun that many a dad took his kids on a picnic to Prestwick's sands and gave them the chance to see the latest flying machines at close quarters.

The airport has had a long American connection and during the Second World War transatlantic flights and air ferry operations were controlled from it, partially by the US Air Force base set up by the Military Air Transport Service. This meant also that large numbers of politicians and assorted VIPs passed through Ayrshire. Prestwick had been an RAF airbase from the thirties till 2013 when operations moved to RAF Swanwick in Hampshire. During the war there were various reorganisations of air traffic control based in and around Prestwick involving a combination of British, Canadian and American controllers mostly working from Redbrae House, previously privately owned, near the current main terminal. The control room was far from that portrayed in modern films and TV where everyone is in headsets and staring at moving dots on a multitude of screens. In the heyday of operations at Redbrae a huge blackboard and plenty of chalk was at the heart of things. Unsophisticated to the modern eye but the folk who work here performed vital roles.

Ambitious plans were drawn up for the post-war era that included a harbour for seaplanes and float planes, but the decline in such traffic meant it never happened, as did a plan to extend the runway to almost four miles long. But unlike Edinburgh and Glasgow, airports Prestwick did have a rail link almost from the start. The US base closed in 1966 but the American connection lingers on in a plaque claiming to mark the fact that the only time Elvis Presley set foot in the UK was in Ayrshire. It is supposed to have happened when Elvis was in the US military and on a transit flight. I like the story but am disappointed to have to record that the claim is contested. Showbiz sources have recently claimed that the King was in London on the day he was supposed to have lounged around Prestwick waiting for a refuelling. Myth or not I like the original story better.

From 1983 BA stopped using the airport which began a period of decline. Other famous names that quit Ayrshire included Pan Am, KLM, SAS, Air Canada and Northwest Orient. The airport was a casualty of improving aircraft performance, including developments in instrumentation that made flying less dependent on weather. Prestwick declined in the early 1980s despite retaining the status of Scotland's transatlantic gateway, which was mostly due to the efforts of local MP, George Younger. Before 1990 every transatlantic flight originating from a Scotland, including Glasgow and Edinburgh, had to touch down at Prestwick before heading out over the ocean. This seriously held aviation in the country in general back.

An example of how irritating this could be is illustrated on a trip around this time I made to North America on Flyglobespan. This relatively short-lived airline had been started by Tom Dalrymple as a short haul tour operator to popular tourist destinations in Europe, but for a while flew to the US and Canada in cooperation with Air Transat, an American operator. On the day I travelled with them I took a taxi from East Renfrewshire to Glasgow to catch the train to Edinburgh and another taxi to Turnhouse. On the Flyglobespan plane we flew across central Scotland at low altitude for fifteen minutes or so to Prestwick. We disembarked there while we waited for some passengers from the south to arrive to join us on the transatlantic flight. Then we trudged back on the plane. By the time we lifted off and headed out over the ocean I felt I had already had enough travel for one day. It was a nonsense especially as Michael Bishop of British Midland had applied as far back as 1982 to operate a Glasgow to Chicago route and been awarded a licence. BAA, the owners of Prestwick successfully objected and the decision was overturned. But it was not until 1990 that Glasgow got transatlantic flights.

Prestwick started as a training airport and it still has a role in this field of aviation. Even trainee *Concorde* pilots got to know it well and golfers on the many courses surrounding the airport and holiday makers on the nearby beaches are well used to the sight of military pilots and commercial pilots on circuit training in various types of aircraft. If no Heathrow or Chicago O'Hare, it still is a mecca for plane spotters. Boeing's *Dreamliner* made its first landing in Scotland here. And a few years ago, on the way home from a few holes of golf, I saw the world's heaviest aircraft – *the Russia Antonov 225* – laboriously haul itself into the sky after collecting freight bound for the States. In military mode this huge plane once carried four tanks weighing almost 250 tonnes. This lifting capacity has made it able to transport emergency supplies to help disaster relief work worldwide. Sadly the only existing *225* was destroyed in the Ukraine war.

Apart from its more than seventy years connection with the RAF, Prestwick had a strong connection with the Royal Navy. On the fringe of the airport itself there was a naval air station called HMS Gannet which hosted helicopters performing military and civilian search and rescue, saving hundreds of lives in sorties from Prestwick out into the wilds of the Atlantic and round the Western Isles or to performing dangerous mountain rescues. In its final years, before the desk-bound politicians in London decided in 2016 to transfer search and rescue to private hands working with the coastguards, the choppers of HMS Gannet were featured on several TV documentaries.

In recent years the airport itself has been something of a political football. It has suffered from a loss of passenger traffic as major companies like BA and SAS closed operations there and budget airlines had to compete with the growth of scheduled and holiday traffic from nearby Glasgow, which had millions spent on improving it after the closure of the old Renfrew airport and presents a glossy new face to travellers. But there is hope for the future. In popular culture space is lauded as "the final frontier". Maybe in Scotland it could be the "new frontier". And it looks as if the technological "covered wagons" are heading for Prestwick and Sutherland. The UK Space Agency and Highland and Islands Enterprise have announced funding for a spaceport in Sutherland. The idea, which is controversial in the area, is to build facilities in the A' Mhòine peninsula for the vertical launch of small satellites. Around the time the Sutherland project became public, it was announced by Prestwick airport that the UK agency was being supportive of their plan to host a horizontal launch site – a concept that has high flying aircraft launching spaceplanes. Scotland has already a burgeoning space development industry that could play a role in the future of communications which could involve "swarms" of small satellites. More of this in the final chapter.

11

Famous Numbers and Never to be Forgotten Heroes

Two the most redolent numbers in the story of Scottish aviation are 602 and 603 – the RAF squadrons of Glasgow and Edinburgh. Equally evocative as the numbers are the names of such as Archie McKellar, George Pinkerton, and Sandy Johnstone under whose leadership more than eighty enemy aircraft were destroyed, the second highest score achieved by Fighter Command. Al Deere was another among those who led the Glasgow flight of *Spitfires* and aces of Edinburgh like Brian Cadbury, Paddy Gilroy and Joe Dalley. Many books and films have been made telling the story of these young men who piloted the legendary *Spitfire* and *Hurricane* fighters. Their courage and skill are in retrospect truly astonishing. Some were barely out of school when they took part in the Battle of Britain. They came from many parts of Britain and what was then called the Empire. Their backgrounds were as diverse as their characters. Many died in combat. One who survived into the jet age was a young New Zealander called Al Deere who led

602 among other postings. He was awarded the Distinguished
Flying Cross in June 1940. His medal was presented to him by
King George VI and the citation was written in unemotional
style. It listed the early "kills" of this fighter ace and told of
remarkable adventures, and crash landings. After one he
walked from Belgium to Dunkirk, managed to get on a Dover
boat, took the train to London and was back with his squadron
less than twenty-four hours after being forced to land on an
enemy-held beach. Another incident caught my eye with enormous force. It was a remarkable illustration of the bravery of
those young RAF pilots. Along with another pilot Deere flew
from a base in the south of England escorting a training aircraft
to a landing spot near Calais on a mission to rescue a squadron
commander who had been shot down. On the return flight the
British planes had just taken off when they were attacked by no
less than twelve *Messerschmitt 109*s (the pre-eminent German
fighter of the day). Deere and his colleague did not run for
it, they attacked the Nazi aircraft and beat them off, shooting
three of them down, severely damaging another three and still
managing to make it home.

Al Deere after the war had a long and successful RAF career
before dying of cancer aged seventy-eight. It is interesting
to note his affection for the "Spit". The three great fighter
planes of the era were, of course, the *Hurricane*, *Spitfire* and
Messerschmit 109. The air aces of the Second World War had
their favourites. Many aviation buffs have tended to favour
the notion that the *Luftwaffe* machine was the best of the three.
This was not the opinion of Al Deere who had cut his teeth
in the *Gloster Gladiator*s (the RAF's last biplane fighter) of 54
Squadron before it converted to the *Spitfire*. Deere said the
"Spit" was the "most beautiful and easy to fly" aircraft. Later
in his service he was given the chance to pilot a captured

109 and found the *Spitfire* superior. In a written report on air combat, he wrote:

"In my opinion the *Spitfire* was superior overall to the *Me 109*, except in the initial climb and dive; however, this was an opinion contrary to the belief of so-called experts. Their judgement was of course based on intelligence assessments and the performance of the *109* in combat with the *Hurricane* in France. In fact, the *Hurricane*, though vastly more manoeuvrable than either the *Spitfire* or the *Me 109*, was sadly lacking in speed and rate of climb, that it's too-short combat experience against the *109* was not a valid yardstick for comparison. The *Spitfire*, however, possessed these two attributes to such a degree, that coupled with a better rate of turn than the *109*, it had the edge in overall combat. There may have been scepticism by some about my claim for the *Spitfire*, but I had no doubts on the score; nor did my fellow pilots in 54 Squadron."

That, to mind settles the old argument. But considering I have never piloted anything not made of balsa wood covered with tissue paper and powered by an engine the size of an egg cup, maybe that doesn't count for much.

A more authoritative assessment of the *Spitfire, Hurricane and Messerschmitt* is contained on the recently published *Battle of Britain* by Simon Pearson and Ed Gorman. They point out that BOTH the legendary British fighters had their faults. The *Spitfire* used a carburettor which could cause a stall in certain conditions. The *Me 109*, however, used a fuel injection system. One major flaw in the design of the *Hurricane* was the proximity of the fuel tanks to the cockpit which meant the pilot was in danger of dying in an inferno. No doubt, too, that the Nazi fliers could pick a fault or two in their own planes. Interestingly Pearson and Gorman point out in their excellent book that the RAF pilots would relax on the ground with a pint or two in the mess while the opponents who waited in the sky for deadly combat were more likely to have been prescribed by Luftwaffe medics a crystal meth type of drug, Pervitan, which could cause addiction, paranoia and depression. Before leaving the *Hurricane, Spitfire, 109* debate it might be pertinent to mention that you will find American air historians who will say that the *P51 Mustang* was a match for any of them in the dogfighting stakes.

There is a sadness in the story of one of Deere's fellow commanders of 602. Archie McKellar was, aptly considering the path his short life was to take, born in Paisley just a short hop in a plane from the military airfield at Abbotsinch. He was schooled at Shawlands Academy in Glasgow. On leaving this highly regarded southside establishment he seemed headed for a career in finance when he took a job with a local stockbroker. But it was soon obvious that such an adventurous spirit was not suitable "bean counting" material and he left to work in his father's construction business as a plasterer, without receiving any favours as the son of the boss. He was one of the guys. When not in dusty white overalls he was a bit of a keep-fit fanatic and, when not at work, a natty dresser, a habit he stuck with in the RAF. His favoured reading was centred round sport, not surprising in "fitba" daft Glasgow, and tales of the First World War flying aces.

The interest in war and the biplane "stringbags" of the era spurred him on to join the Scottish Flying Club which had been founded in 1927 and operated out of nearby Renfrew. "Shrimp" as his RAF pals called him (he was only five feet three tall) was a natural in a cockpit. Lord Clydesdale who was at the time the Commanding Officer of the 602 Squadron of the Auxiliary Air

Force saw an air ace in the making and he invited the young Glaswegian to join. Unlike many of the Battle of Britain young Turks, McKellar was an experienced pilot in the years leading up to the war. The comparison with motor racing stars is often made by aviation historians and seems valid. Had the war not intervened it seems likely that many of the restless and adventurous pilots would have found themselves in a *Ferrari* or a *Maserati* rather than a *Spitfire* or *Hurricane*.

One attribute much needed by racer, or pilot, is good eyesight. Jackie Stewart, that Scottish legend of the track, was so blessed with exceptional vision that it is said that when driving in the *Indianapolis 500* he could pick out friends in the crowd as he sped past. Jackie, too, was a world class clay pigeon shooter. Not so Archie McKellar, who when in training as a flyer was found to have exceptional eyesight. It worked for the air ace in aerial combat, but with a rifle in his hand he was less successful and deemed well below average by the air force. The Auxiliary Air Force in the west of Scotland was based at Abbotsinch in the late thirties and Archie McKellar was part of a voluntary group of part-time reservists, fliers and ground staff, who worked weekends and evenings and had an annual summer fortnight's camp.

The main aircraft at this time was a light bomber, the *Hawker Hind*, but with all-out war fast approaching the Squadron was equipped with the *Spitfire* and moved to RAF bases at Grange-mouth and Drem on the east coast. The unit was charged with defending Edinburgh, Leith, the Forth Bridge and naval targets at Rosyth and the Firth of Forth generally. And it was from there that "Shrimp" was to make history along with George Pinkerton, also to become a 602 legend. The *Spitfires* were called into action. The fear that the closeness of Scotland's east coast to Luftwaffe bases on the continent and the risk of bombing raids had not been overestimated. As early as October, 1939 a flight of around fifteen *Ju 88*s launched an attack on targets around Edinburgh and Rosyth unaware of *Spitfires* in the area. Two of the 602 *Spitfires*, scrambled to take them on, flown by McKellar and George Pinkerton and joined by fighters from 603 Squadron. A mighty air battle resulted. The Germans were led by a noted pre-war airman, Helmut Pohle, who as a test pilot had helped develop the *Ju 88*.

The bombers were after HMS Hood, but the "Mighty Hood" was in dry dock at Roysth, rather than at anchor in the Firth. And strange as it seems, given the way the war was to develop with merciless raids on civilians, Hitler had given orders on this occasion not to attack non-military targets. So, only a cruiser and a destroyer positioned offshore were bombed, and only one navy man was killed. In the process of dropping his bombs, Pohle's cockpit canopy came adrift and he turned northwards over the Firth of Forth but was followed by the Spitfires and shot down. It was to be the first downing of an enemy aircraft during the Second World War. Pohle was the first German prisoner of war in World War Two. His crewmen died but he survived the crash and was imprisoned for a time in Edinburgh Castle and died post war.

Both Pinkerton and McKellar claimed the kill and today there is still controversy about it with some accounts claiming the shot that brought Pohle down came from a *"Spit"* from 603 squadron. Though Pinkerton always said he had fired the shot. Other post-war sources gave the honour to McKellar. Interestingly the Commander-in-Chief of Fighter Command sent a message to 602 saying "Well done, first blood to the auxiliaries", apparently without mentioning anyone by name. The RAF was unable to verify any claim owing to a breakdown in radio communications at the time of the air battle. So the fog of war means that there is no certainty on which pilot brought Pohle down. It all seems a bit academic now – the *Spitfires* had done the job and the Germans who called the area around the Firth of Forth "suicide alley" had had a taste of what was to come in the Battle of Britain. Later the dogfights ahead over the skies around London gave Archie McKellar the chance to, along with Ronald Hamlyn and Brian Carbury, gain the accolade "Ace in a Day" for shooting down five *Me 109*s in twenty-four hours.

His feat was accomplished on October 7, 1940, almost a year to the day after that fateful battle over the Firth of Forth. Indeed, most of his "kills" were accomplished in a brief period before he was shot down and killed on the first day after the official end of the Battle of Britain, November 1, 1940. It was typical for one of the great aces of that battle, that he had taken off to engage a whole flight of attackers. It is thought he brought one enemy plane down before fate caught up with him. It may have been a short combat career, but it was sensationally successful. The "Shrimp" too became a giant of aerial combat with a total of twenty-two accredited victories and other shared kills. The debate about *Hurricane* v *Spitfire*, mentioned earlier, did not matter much to this brave Scot; he flew both types with great skill to contribute significantly to defeating Germany. George Pinkerton, a scion of a notable west of Scotland farming family, who was educated at Glasgow's famous high school in the fashionable west end, survived the war and died in his eighties.

Another 602 legend was Paddy Finucane who died aged twenty-one when shot down off the coast of occupied France, near Le Touquet, in the summer of 1942. He was of English heritage, born in County Dublin, and grew up in the troubled days of the thirties before the family moved back to England in 1936 where he joined the RAF in 1938. Wing Commander Brendon Eamonn Fergus Finucane, DSO, DFC & Two Bars, to give him his Sunday name was a popular character. But unlike Pinkerton and McKellar, despite his enthusiasm for flying he was not a natural. The concept of motor racing stars in the cockpit could be used again in the case of Paddy. But he had a different style to some of the other air aces. Aficionados of motor sport thought there were two types of drivers; the guys who pulled down the goggles and "put pedal to metal", wresting their machines in a series of power slides and the others who drove smoothly and unspectacularly, but deceptively fast. In a car Finucane would have been in the first category.

His training did not go smoothly and his learning period was marked with at least one crash-landing and various incidents. Yet it was a different story after he gained his wings. Promotions came quickly and in January 1942 he was made Squadron Leader of 602. After a mere six months further service in action he became the youngest wing commander in the history of the RAF. As with some of the other aces of the war, the exact total of his kills can't be completely accurate, but some historians put it as high as thirty-two, including twenty-three *Messerschmitt 109s* and four *Focke-Wulf 190s*. Some contribution to the war effort.

Obviously 603 City of Edinburgh Squadron, too, played a major role in the war in the air. Just like the cities of Glasgow and Edinburgh themselves, there has always been great, if good natured and friendly, rivalry between the two sets of fliers. Frankly, looking back to the great histories of both squadrons, and the men who lost their lives, it seems to me that, as my dad would have said, "comparisons are odious". The courage of young men from many parts of Britain and the Commonwealth can never be disregarded. Their contribution to winning the Second World War and turning the tide at the time of the Battle of Britain, cannot be underestimated and should not be forgotten.

The bald figures, looking back around eighty years, are remarkable. Officially the air battle in the skies of southern England started on July 10, 1940 and ended on October 31, the same year: just under 3,000 British, Commonwealth, and Allied aircrew took part in the fighting. The average age of the pilots in what became known as "the few" in the Battle of Britain, was twenty-two. The bravery of these men, many from privileged backgrounds who could have looked forward to a gilded life, is truly remarkable. As is the fact that one in three of the men who climbed into a fighter cockpit and took to the air in combat with the Luftwaffe was either killed or wounded. Many who survived were badly burned. Edinburgh's 603 had been moved south after those initial skirmishes over the Firth of Forth and found itself at the centre of a defining part of the conflict.

A goodly proportion of the aces of 603 came from legal or minor aristocratic families. They were the sort of guys brought up in the well-heeled areas of the prosperous capital in the late thirties. Normally they were the types who pulled on the string driving gloves and headed the MG to the nearest point-to-point or elite golf club. You could have categorised them as "tearaways" with class – but when the chips were down they changed from holding up the bars of expensive aero clubs into well-trained brave pilots equal or better than any who flew in planes smeared with the swastika. Mostly flying from RAF Hornchurch in the Battle of Britain, 603 Squadron shot down fifty-seven enemy aircraft which was more than double the other flights of *Spitfires*. They had forty-seven pilots taking part in the battle and lost thirteen. As I said comparison can be odious, but they can also be revealing. Modern estimates indicate, though no figures on the battle can be totally accurate, that the Luftwaffe lost around two and a half thousand pilots and the RAF figure was nearer five hundred. No doubt then who the victors were. But it wasn't just the fliers. The ground crews played a great role in the battle, servicing the planes for a quick turnaround and repairing bullet holes as well keeping the complex engines in tip-top order. These guys knew the pilots well and watched the take-off anxiously . . . How many would come back?

One of the 603 legends was Brian Carbury, who recorded fifteen kills, the first days after the move to England. The RAF was big on nicknames and Carbury's mess moniker was "Rasp Berry". Carbury was back in Scotland briefly at the end of 1940 and celebrated Christmas day that fateful year by damaging a *Junkers 88* which had strayed into air space around St Abb's Head. In 1943 the squadron was switched to the Middle East. Around the same time one of the stalwarts, Flight Sergeant, Joe Dalley, flew from England to Malta to become one of four pilots to be based there who became known as the "eyes and ears" of the beleaguered little island.

At end of the war in 1945 the squadron was disbanded but reformed a year later to fly from RAF Turnhouse, Edinburgh's civil airport. When in 1957 it was disbanded again the squadron was flying *Vampire* jets. A lot had happened to aircraft design since 603 had been formed – primitive *Westland Wapitis* (named after a breed of elk for some reason), a single engine general purpose biplane with a top speed of 130 mph, was for a while a stalwart. Others in the pre-*Spitfire* era were the *Hawker Hart* and the *Gloster Gladiator*. Somewhat different from the *Vampire*. Edinburgh and Glasgow folk driving between Scotland's two main cities are familiar with the sight, and noise of big passenger jets taking off and landing on the runway of the capital's airport as it is close to the A8 and the M8 motorway. So close that when the *Vampires* were first posted north, there was a worry about what would happen if a military fighter failed to lift off before it ran out of runway. The Royal Navy helped the Royal Air Force out and catch netting, like that used on aircraft carriers, was stretched across the final yards of runway. Fortunately, it was never used! But it was an ingenuous idea.

12

Swastikas, Spies and Clydebank Ablaze

The wings that flew over Scotland didn't always feature the familiar, comforting, RAF roundel or the attractive colourful livery of a favourite airline. The Lufthansa *Junkers* that transported the German soccer team into the old Renfrew airport in the years before World War Two started, sporting the swastika, was in a few years replaced by more sinister products of the skilled aircraft manufacturing industry of the Nazis – *Messerschmitt* bombers and fighters, *Dorniers*, *Focke-Wulfs*, *Heinkels*, and other less well-known craft. From my early years growing up in Glasgow I can remember the frightening drone of squadrons flouting the swastika flying in from the east determined to destroy Scotland's industrial capacity and attempting to bomb the civilian population into submission. Including me, as the late Spike Milligan might have said.

Young as I was, I vaguely remember crossing the back garden to the relative safety of the corrugated iron Anderson shelter, dug into our vegetable patch, and glancing upwards at the spectacular display of searchlights probing the sky for the unseen enemy preparing to drop ton-upon-ton of high explosives on factories, schools, churches, shipyards hospitals and housing. But I do remember, too, sing-songs in that shelter, with the neighbours and their children waiting for the sound of the "all clear" sirens and a return to a warm bed. Even a child could detect a natural feeling of communal anxiety mixed with a sense of determination not to be beaten. My experience was tiny and insignificant compared with that of Londoners sheltering in sleeping bags deep in the tube or Clydebankies emerging into the rubble that once had been a town after the great Blitz of March 13 and 14, 1941. Hitler had miscalculated if he believed that the resolve of the British could be broken by bombs. Indeed, most historians think that the savagery of that night in Clydebank, Greenock and parts of the Central Belt had the opposite effect.

The folk of Clydebank epitomised that great spirit. And their actions during the actual nights of the bombing and the aftermath were heroic and "beyond praise" as it was put by the many historians of the nights of the raids. Civilian air raid wardens played an important rescue role during appalling carnage. This was the worst destruction and civilian loss of life in Scotland in the Second World War. The bald facts are horrendous – around 1,000 people died, 1,000 were seriously injured and hundreds of others had injuries from blast and falling debris. Out of 12,000 houses only eight were undamaged. Thirty-five thousand were made homeless. An astonishing 439 bombers took part in the raids and dropped more than 1,000 bombs, a mixture of incendiaries and high explosives. It is said that at the height of the attack pilots of planes in the Aberdeen area could see the blaze reflected in the clouds. Clydebank has a memorial to the "bankies" who died, and the total figure of fatalities, not just in the shipyard town is related to the rogue acts of German pilots. The main targets on the first night were obviously such as John Brown, Beardmores, Denny's, the huge Singer sewing machine factory and other industrial enterprises packed into a tiny area of Clydeside. And the fact that most of the workers in Clydebank lived more or less "above the shop" in densely populated tenement buildings added immensely to the death toll.

The town was not well defended. RAF planes shot down only two of the armada of planes that attacked. Despite many anti-aircraft gun sites on the neighbouring hills, none were shot down by them. But the ground-based guns did influence the German pilots. Realising the amount of anti-aircraft fire around the key sites, some prematurely dropped their bombs short of the real target and headed for home. Craters left by the air armada were found miles out in the country, something that suggests that maybe a significant number of Herr Hitler's aviators were not, as they say, "truly made of the right stuff". But their colleagues who pressed on to bomb the targets selected by the Nazi high command left a stain on humanity that will not be forgotten.

In memoirs of the World War Two bombing not enough attention, in my opinion, is given to raids on Scotland other than Edinburgh, Glasgow and industrial Lanarkshire. It is recorded that Peterhead was bombed twenty-eight times, Aberdeen twenty-four and Fraserburgh twenty-three. Even Montrose was attacked from the air more times than Glasgow. Not that all these places played a vital war role – the reason is that if you were a Nazi pilot flying west from Norway the east coast towns were the first areas of population, and easy targets, before a 180 degree turn, scuttling back across the North Sea to safety.

A couple of months after the appalling disaster of the Clydebank Blitz the Luftwaffe was again flouting the swastika over the Renfrewshire hills, on the western side of the

Clyde. No massive air armada this time, just the drone of a single *Messerschmitt 110*. Normally this aircraft, a twin-engined fighter/bomber was designed to have a crew of two or three and was a pet project of Hermann Goering, who in the late thirties saw it as a vital item in the armoury of the Luftwaffe whose expansion he masterminded. The *110* was an interesting design with Daimler Benz engines that could let it reach more than 300 mph. This was fast for the time and in some configurations it was speedier than early model RAF *Hurricanes*, although the failings of the *110* were exposed in the Battle of Britain when it was no match for the more agile *Hurricanes* and *Spitfires*. Despite the backing of Goering, like many a compromise, it was neither the best fighter nor the best bomber.

But this was of little significance on the night of May 10, 1941 when that lone *110* was spotted, its engine sounding distinctly dodgy as it lumbered over the Glasgow southside suburb of Busby, heading towards the historic village of Eaglesham a few miles away. It was nearing midnight, but with double summertime in operation the skies were relatively clear. If the locals feared being bombed they need not have worried. This *Messerschmitt* had no bombs, no crew of three, just a lone flier. And his mission was apparently "peace" not war. The stuttering of the *110*'s powerful engines was caused by fuel failure after a nearly 1,000-mile flight zigzagging from Bavaria. The plane crash-landed in a field on the outskirts of Eaglesham. Some reports at the time claimed the pilot had parachuted out before the landing, but that may have been because he was retrieving his chute when a local ploughman, David McLean, appeared, according to reports, pitchfork in hand. The downed flier was no ordinary Luftwaffe fighter jockey, this was no less than Rudolph Hess, deputy to the Fuhrer Adolf Hitler himself.

Hess had escaped from the descent unhurt though conflicting reports in the newspapers of the time variously said he had broken an ankle or that he walked into the arms of the Home Guard with a limp. What happened that moonlit Renfrewshire night started a controversy that lasted almost fifty years. The immediate rumour was that the pilot who had landed at Floors farm was not really Hess, but a lookalike pretending to be Hess. The flier may have helped cause this by telling the locals he was Hauptmann Alfred Horn, though he later admitted to the authorities he was Hess. Why he did not immediately say he was Hess is a mystery that, like some other parts of the story of Rudolph Hess' Scottish misadventure, is unexplained. No matter, the German was marched, presumably at the end of that pitchfork, by the local farmer to his house and the Home Guard informed. A detachment of the Royal Signals, based nearby, also arrived on the scene and Hess handed over his pistol to the soldiers who had no firearms.

The mysterious German was taken to the Busby HQ of the Home Guard, a few miles from where the *Messerschmitt* had landed, where the local bush telegraph had informed the populace that something big was happening and a curious crowd surrounded the building. An eyewitness told the *Daily Record* that the crowd waited a couple of hours while Hess languished inside. The onlookers got more than they bargained for as instead of the Army lorry with a few soldiers they had expected to take the captive to Maryhill Barracks, on the other side of the river, a stream of high-ranking officers in staff cars descended on the village. This was clearly a matter of importance.

Interestingly, when Hess, still in his aviator's gear, left the building, if he had a broken ankle it was well disguised and not remarked on by locals. The Busby folk went home to bed rather surprised that their little suburban hideaway was at the centre of an international news story. What was Hess doing in Scotland? He had not arrived there by accident, a stray pilot who lost his way. This was far from the case – Hess' flight was a carefully planned exploit. It is often overlooked that the Fuhrer's Deputy was a lauded pre-war aviator who had won at least one important air race. Perhaps aware that high level involvement in Nazi politics had left his flying skills a tad rusty, his training for a meticulously planned flight to Scotland included lessons from *Messerschmitt*'s chief test pilot Wilhelm Stor. They used a specific *110* that handled well and was held in reserve for Hess's personal use. He logged many training cross-country flights in this period and had the plane's oxygen delivery system modified and a radio compass installed along with large long-range fuel tanks. This was no quick jump in a plane and pop over to Scotland flight. Several early planned trips were cancelled owing to weather but at 17.45 the modified 110 took off with the Deputy Fuhrer at the controls in a flying suit bearing the rank of captain. He took money, toiletries, a torch, camera, maps and charts and a selection of twenty-eight different medicines (plus some homeopathic remedies) plus dextrose to keep him awake. After crossing the North Sea, he was spotted by a warning station near Newcastle and two *Spitfires* were sent to intercept him but failed, as did a third fighter that was sent to hunt him. By now he was flying so low and fast to throw off defenders that a *Boulton Paul Defiant* from Prestwick also failed to intercept him. No doubt by now tired and confused by the cat-and-mouse nature of his flight he was running out of fuel and crash-landed. He was a mere twelve miles from his intended destination – Dungavel House. The mysteries and controversies deepened.

Why was this summer retreat of the Duke of Hamilton, of Everest fame, the target? The truth of the matter is hidden in the swirling haze of Nazi high politics. One fact though is that the Duke of Hamilton was not, as Hess claimed, in any way willing to do a deal with Hitler to end the war. Hess had given an associate a letter to give to Hitler telling of his, Hess', intention to open peace negotiations with the British. On reading this Hitler had one of his near berserk outbursts fearing an attempt to depose him. The Fuhrer thought that Japan and Italy would think he was secretly trying to negotiate a peace. The German press was told to portray Hess as a deranged madman, his judgement and mental health affected by old war injuries. Hess was stripped of all authority and ordered to be shot on sight if he returned to Germany. Another complication was that Stalin was suspicious that Britain was involved though Churchill later wrote that Hess crossed to Britain by his own free will.

While all this was causing immediate international confusion back in Glasgow, in the dour surrounding of Maryhill barracks, Hess was held and interrogated. He was also for a while in the beautiful surrounding of Buchanan Castle on the shores of Loch Lomond. (One of his guards at the time was Willie Ross who went on to be Scottish Secretary.) By now he had confirmed that he was indeed the Deputy Fuhrer. The Duke of Hamilton had a meeting down south with Churchill to report on the events and destroy Hess' peacemaking claims and to plan Britain's next move to smooth over an incident that was troubling to the Allies. An amusing aside to this is that on arrival in London the wartime premier was watching a Marx Brothers film and the Duke had to wait till it was over before getting to tell the story of Hess' arrival in Scotland.

After the initial interrogations, Hess was moved south and held in the Tower of London, but emerged, still with his head in place, to face trial at Nuremburg in 1946. Unlike many of his former Nazi colleagues he escaped execution and ended up in

Spandau Prison in Berlin where he committed suicide at the age of ninety-three. The many years of his incarceration were thick with controversy and there were even theories that his death was not suicide but murder. How this notion got any traction at all is hard to fathom – why wait from 1946 to kill him in 1987? During those long years of captivity regular rumours persisted that the man in the cell was an imposter, not the Fuhrer's former deputy. One long running proponent of the theory was a British surgeon working in Germany who claimed the man known as "Prisoner 7" in Spandau did not show any signs of scarring from old wounds that the real Hess would have exhibited. This is the only smidgeon of evidence to support the imposter theory. But what must be set against it is the undoubted fact that in the dock at Nuremburg the many Nazis, waiting for a date with the hangman, seemed to treat Hess as the man they knew. And in Spandau he was visited by relatives who also accepted he was who he said he was.

A former colleague of mine, the celebrated author Jack Webster, who has written extensively on the case and is a shrewd observer, was in no doubt what was the truth. In his book *The Flying Scots*, he wrote:

"Having met some of those propagating the theories, however, I came to suspect the power of fertile imagination was a factor".

That imagination rumbled on for years producing fanciful stories that the use of an imposter was to cover up all sorts of difficult to believe notions of secret plots involving Hitler, Russia and even Churchill. While it is true that Hess' motives for that strange flight to Scotland might never be fully explained the identity of "Prisoner 7" is now not in doubt. In 2019, DNA testing by Sherman McCall, of the prestigious American military Walter Reed Medical

Center, and Jan Cemper-Kiesslich, a researcher at the University of Salzburg, demonstrated a 99.99 per cent match between the man in Spandau's "Y" chromosome DNA markers and those of a living Hess relative. Case closed. At least one part of it!

An interesting sidebar to the Hess tale is something seldom mentioned in connection with the mystery. The field where Hess' plane crashed was extremely close to one of Glasgow's "Starfish" sites – decoy areas designed to lure the Luftwaffe bombers away from the city's industrial areas and the Clydeside shipyards. Highly secret at the time, the decoy operation was to build elaborate arrays of lights simulating streets or airfields and fires that from the air would look like burning cities or towns. The sites were controlled from bomb-proof bunkers. Glasgow had two decoy targets, one on each side of the Clyde, one near Eaglesham, East Renfrewshire, and the other on the east side of the city at Craigmaddie on the Campsie Fells. The Eaglesham one still shows evidence of where the basket fires once stood and fire-break trenches. It was not a one-off bright idea to confuse the Nazi pilots – by the end of the war 237 decoys around the country were built to protect eighty-one towns and cities. Some estimates suggest that around 1,000 tons of German bombs were dropped on the decoys, saving British lives.

There is another aspect of the story that might have non-aviation buffs thinking ... How come the good folk of Busby, Lanarkshire, could be certain enough of what kind of plane Hess flew over the village that late night in 1941? The answer might be something of a surprise to modern readers – the now largely forgotten prevailing influence in the Second World War of the Royal Observer Corps. This organisation from 1925 to 1957 trained civilians and military personnel in aircraft recognition. These days the design, particularly, of large passenger jets has developed to the point that only those with a taste for anoraks and notebooks can tell one plane from another. At the start of the Second World War the Air Ministry thought that, however desirable it might be, recognising the various types of planes that flew high and fast was not possible. They were proved wrong by organisations such as the Royal Observer Corps Club and its magazine called, without much sign of imagination, *The Aeroplane Spotter*. This enthusiastic mix of amateur aviation buffs and the military produced posters galore and booklets illustrated by silhouettes of various types of aircraft. As a Boy Scout in the years after the war I saw many of these guides to recognition and they were almost works of art showing in black and white what were called the WEFT characteristics (Wing shape, Engine configuration, Fuselage shape, and Tail type). During the war there were 30,000 spotters in the Corps, an astonishing number. They certainly saved lives with warnings of Luftwaffe planes overhead and they also cut down the friendly fire casualties in the air battles over Britain's skies using their skill to separate friend from foe. And, of course, it also helped if an observer spotting an enemy in the sky could identify the type of craft giving a clue to whether or not it was on a spying mission or a bombing raid.

Incidentally Dungavel House, the target that Hess failed to reach, had an interesting history. These days, with second homes popular, we think nothing of a journey of 100 miles or so to a pad near a beach or up a mountain for a brief getaway. The Hamilton clan when not flying over the top of the world in the Himalayas, or immersed in the social swirl in London, took summer breaks from the luxury of their main home in Hamilton Palace to Dungavel, just a few miles down the road. After the war this property was sold to the National Coal Board before becoming an open prison, something that interested me wearing my other hat as a writer on prison matters. It was here that a remarkable feisty woman called Agnes Curran made history as the country's first woman governor of a male prison. A notorious Glasgow gangster, Walter Norval, did some time in the place and got to know her, and respect her, which is something of a compliment from a guy who served many long years in Scotland's toughest jails. It may have been the first time Walter and his hard men mates had been in a prison where the boss smelled of perfume, but Agnes handled her "guests" with aplomb and paved the way for successors in the prison service. It is perhaps apt, that considering Rudolf Hess' illegal immigrant bid all these years ago, Dungavel is now a detention centre for illegal immigrants. Maybe he just flew in too early . . .

I wonder if when Rudolph Hess languished all these years in Spandau he, as a pre-war distinguished pilot, kept up with the march of German aviation. The national flag carrier, Lufthansa, was founded as far back as 1926 and thrived till the Nazi's surrendered in 1945 when all its services were grounded. A new Lufthansa was formed in 1955 and domestic flights began again, followed by transatlantic service using that beautiful plane the *Constellation*. But it took to the sixties before German aircraft headed again into the skies above Glasgow, this time minus the menacing swastika as a logo. The inaugural post-war service was to the German airline's main base at Frankfurt. To drum up custom for the new route Lufthansa launched a publicity drive including wooing the Scottish press.

The head of the airline's PR operation in London at that time was an elderly German with an aristocratic background and a pre-war history that included close political contact with the German high command. Part of his PR strategy was to take Scottish reporters to the Frankfurt headquarters to see for themselves what a fine job the company was doing in rebuilding the airline. It was a lavish, free jaunt and I was lucky enough to be assigned by the news desk to this not too challenging assignment.

Along with some others hacks we were invited by the PR mastermind to a lunch at Glasgow's famed *Rogano* restaurant which specialised in seafood. It was a high class venue not too familiar with some of the group who gathered before flying to Germany. Naturally we were offered an impressive salver of oysters with the pre-lunch G and Ts. The gin was certainly familiar enough to the Scots, though the oysters were a different story. One unworldly hack inquired whether they should be gulped down or chewed. Our immaculately dressed host, who never clicked his heels in our company but looked as if he would at any moment, replied that "The Fuhrer chewed his . . . " Name dropping with class.

When this group finally got to Germany, we were treated to a tour of pilot training facilities and a visit to Lufthansa's state of the art simulator, something of a novelty then. A pleasant morning was spent with the Scots learning that landing a *Boeing 707* was not as easy as it looked and one by one our attempts ended with the screen going blank and a simulated crash. It was all good fun until one of us asked the chief instructor had he ever flown to Scotland. I knew Clydebank he replied. Suddenly the atmosphere was a tad more sober. In these days buying good publicity for new routes by taking reporters specialising in aviation on flights was common. Nowadays the practice is much more tightly controlled, with travel writers carefully acknowledging who was paying for the five-star hotels and for them to turn left on climbing the stairs (no air bridges then) to enter a plane. But thirty or so years ago it was a touch different. Though I remember from my *Express* days that Lord Beaverbrook, or his management minions, began to play a straight bat, insisting that if we accepted a trip the paper paid the going rate for flights and hotels. It was a healthy development and one journalist turned it to his advantage by insisting his by-line was followed by the words "the man who pays his way".

Looking back there was a lot of fun in these less regulated days and "freebies" were part of a world where journalists toiled over a hot typewriter rather than staring at a screen and hitting spell check every few moments. And airline executives anxious to maximise utilisation of the latest planes never quite understood the rationale for paying for something you were being offered for free. One airline that tended to treat the travel writers well was British Midland. They took a bunch of us from Glasgow to Amsterdam. Oysters were not on the menu this time, but there would have been little room for them anyway after a Dutch twenty-two course dinner of specialities from the East Indies. One well kempt figure on the Glasgow newspaper scene, who remains nameless, won't forget that trip. Entranced by the sight of the city's red-light area's naked shop window sirens, he stepped back for better view, tripped and fell into a canal. The girls put business to one side and called the police to rescue him and take him to hospital for a check-up. A gulp of Amsterdam canal water was not quite as healthy as a sip of Highland Spring.

Other jaunts included a day trip to the Channel Islands which started badly with one of us getting his Ford Fiesta hire car whacked on the head by an overeager car park barrier. It ended worse with a colleague having a couple of cases of duty-free wine taken from him despite declaring it hand luggage. The bargain wine took a week or so to arrive back in the west end and it was accompanied by a hefty bill for carriage. He could have saved his cash and bought it in Byres Road.

13

The Shuttle . . . Turn Up and Go and Champagne by the Tanker Load

In my layman's view one plane changed aviation more than any other in history – the *Douglas DC3 aka* the *Dakota*. The adjective most used to describe this flying legend is "indestructible". But it is also, to this day, a beautiful mechanical object. The comment on the *Concorde* and the *Comet* often made, "if it looks right it flies right", could also be applied to the *Dakota*. It had strong Scottish connections as an early workhorse for British European Airways "BEA" (it stayed in service till 1962), and the old Scottish Airways. It was a familiar sight in Scottish skies for years. So, it is appropriate that the aircraft featured in one of the renowned artist and historian Dugald Cameron's very many magnificent paintings of early aviation is a Pioneer class *DC3* that proudly bore the name "RMA Percy Pilcher". Many books have been written about the "Dak" and stories of its sturdiness are profuse.

The original design, not surprisingly, was based on the Douglas company's *DC1* and 2, the letter "C" was to indicate commercial rather than military. The new planes were planned to break Boeing's grip on passenger aviation in America in the early thirties, a move that was largely successful. The first *DC1* was a single machine that was built to test new theories of design and was never put into volume production. But its gleaming pristine aluminium structure gave a warning to the early world airlines that the era of the *Ford Trimotor* and the popular *Fokker* airliners was under threat. Donald Douglas, the founder of the company that grew to become one of the biggest aircraft building companies in history, was the son of a Brooklyn bank cashier of Scottish descent, maybe the name is a clue. Those Wright brothers are hard to keep out of any flying story and they were the men who set Donald Douglas on the way to fame. As a youngster he had gone to a field in Virginia in 1908 to watch Orville demonstrate a plane for the US Army. He was hooked on flying and the dream that became the Douglas Aircraft Corporation took off.

Right from the start Donald Douglas was insistent of the sort of stress testing that was to lead to the "indestructible *DC3*" – though flying into a mountain at high speed was still not a particularly good idea. After he saw a contemporary designer in the cockpit of one his planes, lifted on wooden plinths, throwing his weight about he asked what was going on and was told: "I am testing it to see if it is strong enough". Douglas twigged that the way ahead was to be a tad more sophisticated. The wings of the early *DC1*, 2 and 3 series, which were of innovative design, were subjected to scientific stress analysis, as were all the other components. To prove the point about the strength of the finished product, journalists were treated to the unscientific sight of a steam road roller driving back and forth over the wings! They flexed as they were intended to in turbulence but were undamaged. This was no meaningless stunt. When in service one *Dakota*, on a pass over mountains in winter, landed with an inch or so of ice on the wings which mechanics reckoned weighed more than a ton.

Strength was not the only virtue of the *Dakota*. Here is what the legendary pilot and aviation writer Ernest K Gann had to say about flying this famed plane: "The 'three' was an amiable cow that was forgiving to the clumsiest pilot." Considering the fine lines of the *DC3*, the only comment to make is that "cow" is to my mind not quite the right word, but you get the drift. The remarkable longevity of this plane was not completely owed to a simple design which prioritised easy maintenance. Some of the credit must also go to the aviation industry's rigidly enforced safety rules and the replacement of out of time parts etc. It is said that when one experienced *Dakota* pilot was asked how much of the original fifty-odd-year-old plane he was flying was "new" he cheekily replied, "I suppose if you looked hard enough you might find a few of the original rivets."

Though the *Dakota* served Scotland well I never travelled in it in my own country. But I did experience it when on assignment in the far north of Canada. In Alaska and Yukon, it was akin to the village bus. To anyone used to turboprops or jets, flying on it was an eye-opener. Its tricycle style landing gear meant that when on the ground you had to walk uphill to get to the front of the plane from seats near the tail. In the air there was much less noise and vibration than you would expect, a factor in its commercial success. The engine noise was vaguely reassuring. In-flight service was basic – a cardboard box with a sandwich or two and a doughnut. No fine wines – just bring your own beer. The food on one flight was brought to me by a woman who was born and brought up in the northwest and it was entertaining to hear the details of her life in this spectacular, mountainous region, where travelling south to the Canadian provinces or the States was referred to as "going outside". This stewardess told me that one of the most exciting days of her life was going as a teenager for the first time into a car. Up north your status could be measured by how many canoes you had moored at your house, not how many cars you had in the garage. For, of course, in a huge land area with virtually no roads, wings were more important that wheels.

In the Yukon you travelled by float plane, a *DC3* or some battered oil-stained old workhorse retired from a busy life "outside" as Douglas and Boeing fought for the biggest share in the fast-growing airline business linking the great North American cities. In Ernest K Gann's "amiable old cow" you felt safe and comfortable as shirt-sleeved pilots chatted over their shoulders with old mates in the way the village bus driver would at home. But the views were rather better than you would get on a bus. The *Dakota* had limited ability at high altitude and when crossing the northern territory wilderness, you often took a winding route in and around the thousands of miles of snow-covered peaks, rather than suffer turbulent air and loss of power by flying over them. The valleys between the mountains were deep and narrow but the bush pilots knew them well and were unconcerned to have steep cliffs that often looked too near for comfort as you trundled sedately from one settlement to another and learned about a different way of life from any native Americans on board ... such as the details of such important matters as how to make maximum use of the carcass of a caribou. I was told with some enthusiasm, that in a country where you must maximise a kill to live, nothing went to waste. Steaks, of course, and skin to make clothing to resist the sub-zero winter temperatures. Bone and sinew went into making skeletons for boats, tents and sewing equipment. Other parts, too sensitive for an impressionable young Scot were also used! Nothing was wasted. Not quite the chat you get from an upper-class stewardess on the old BA.

The *Dakota* certainly looked the part whether lifting off from a strip in Alaska or a wee field in Scotland's Highlands. An equally eye-catching aircraft familiar in the early days of the Scottish airline business was the ubiquitous de Havilland *Rapide*. When launched in the early thirties it was marketed as the *Dragon Rapide* though as it graduated through many variations it became more simply the *Rapide*. In contrast to most of the biplanes of the time, which often had a Heath Robinson look, the *Rapide* had a streamlined style to it. Its looks certainly contributed to it becoming perhaps the most successful short-haul passenger plane of the thirties. In another guise, as the *Dominie*, it did good service with the RAF for years and as an air ambulance. It had a remarkably long life considering it was to a great extent of primitive plywood construction. The *Rapide* (piloted by David Barclay) was used by Northern & Scottish Airways when in 1938 it pioneered a new route from Renfrew via Perth, Inverness, and Kirkwall to Sumburgh. Several surviving *Rapide*s are crowd pullers at aviation museums in many parts of the world. It still looks ahead of its time.

All this is a long way from the normal aviation antics of my early years in journalism which mostly centred around the legendary Glasgow–London shuttle and the occasional trip across the Atlantic for a spot of travel writing. There is one connection – the shuttle idea was copied from American Airlines. The way it worked seems a fantasy now. When British Airways (formed in 1974 with the merger of BEA and BOAC) launched it in 1975 it was called a "turn up and go" service. You turned up at the aircraft gate without a ticket or any documentation ten minutes before take-off time and you were guaranteed a seat. If the plane was full another was ready for you even if you would be the only passenger. I am unsure how often this did actually happen with a solo passenger, but there is no doubt that often a backup shuttle flight left Glasgow for London with a handful of businessmen heading for meetings in England, all being told how to run their companies by public schoolboys who did not know their Epping from their Eriskay (this sour observation was brought on by personal experience!) However, the shuttle was something else – no queues to buy a ticket, no queues to get a boarding pass. It was as easy as getting on a bus. No need either to look up a timetable. Weekdays there were eight flights at fifteen minutes past the hour from 7.15 to 20.15. The return timetable was similar. The idea of having expensive planes on standby rather than passengers waiting for a seat was not welcome to the national airline's independent rivals who were cynical about the taxpayer picking up the tab for such services. And it was only after British Midland came on the Glasgow-Heathrow scene as a rival with a better than adequate cabin service, that BA had to up their game and match their rivals with hot breakfasts and free drinks.

It was undoubtedly a great idea though and BA's advertising copywriters must have thought they had won the lottery when given the chance to publicise such a sure-fire service. The concept and the fact that it really did work made it difficult for the advertising guys to know where to start. One ad had the headline: "On British Airways shuttle the passenger always flies. Only the planes stand-by!" Another ad had a sketch of a refuelling tanker with champagne scrawled against its side drawn up beside a jet in case you had not by now grasped the fact that fizz was consumed in great quantities. One copywriter concentrated rather differently on the safety side of things and I imagine him, or her, almost drooling with pleasure as those travellers more interested on getting to London alive, rather than the amount of complimentary drinks on offer were informed: "In poor visibility the shuttle really comes into its own. It has the advanced category-3 landing equipment on every aircraft. If you believe airports are for flying out of rather than hanging around in, shuttle is the only way to fly." Indeed it was, for a number of years. In its heyday the shuttle had a dedicated fleet of nine *Hawker Siddeley Tridents*. I always enjoyed the *Trident* though that landing equipment, so liked by BA's ad men, had an unsettling effect on passengers as a "blind" landing, as it was called, required much automatic juggling of throttles and what can only be described as a "shoogly" approach to the tarmac. But it did work even in heavy fog and wild Scottish, sleety, November crosswinds.

The *Trident* is undoubtedly the plane most associated with the shuttle but after the early years, the *Boeing 757* took over from the aging British *Tri-jet* and in turn the *Boeing* was replaced by the significantly smaller *Airbus 320*. Started before the era of cheapo airlines like easyJet and Ryanair, which only came along in the nineties, and competing on the Glasgow–London route with British Midland, BA in the early days went heavy on cabin service. One of the joys at the start of the shuttle was to watch the cabin crew fighting the clock to get the meal service completed before the descent into Heathrow. It is interesting to look back forty years or so and realise how the perception of the job of stewardess, aka cabin attendant, has changed.

Once this was considered a glamorous occupation, smart uniform, heavy use of make-up and the chance to visit faraway places. On the shuttle the reality was rather different – after arduous lengthy training, including safety procedures, you ended up with the daily slog of serving meal after meal, and drink after drink, in a hectic burst of controlled chaos trying to beat the clock before the next landing. Or maybe it would be flight after flight to one of the Costas with a plane-load of holidaymakers, the adrenaline flowing in anticipation of a fortnight in the sun and with many of the adults tanked up after drinking sessions in the airport bars which started serving pints as soon as the sun rose. The far from political correctness of the time could mean a bit of name calling, though to be fair some of it was light-hearted. To be called a cart tart or a trolley dolly was dismissed with a contemptuous smile and a flick of the ponytail. Babies and young children who seemed to have been trained to enjoy kicking in the back of the seat added more stress, and even the pilots had extra worries on such flights. Not everyone coming home from Spain wore a sombrero and carried a straw donkey, though plenty did, but the holiday cases were rather fuller on the return than on the way down to the Med. The extra weight of a return flight had to be factored into the flight plan.

Long-haul flying was, however, slightly more glamorous and less taxing. The rush here was to get the nasty business of serving dinner over and the movie on as quickly as possible. And at the first opportunity to dim the cabin lights and get back to the meal preparation area as fast as possible for the opportunity to gossip whilst the over-refreshed passengers dosed. But if bound for Singapore or Australia there was always the prospect of a stopover in a decent-ish hotel as crews changed over. The time spent waiting for another long-haul home was not wasted. G and Ts poolside were in order and many a romance blossomed between cabin crews and pilots waiting for the next flight.

This was at least a touch of glamour. British airlines generally liked the girls to be youngish. Not so, the Americans who let some cabin attendants spend a working life in the air, still flying after sixty-five. Those who did became wise old birds. I remember a flight, with some other young scribes, from Los Angeles to Honolulu, being served by a stewardess who could have been our granny. One look at us and she remarked, "I guess you lot would like a few extra plastic cups." The rules said no drinking of passengers' own carry-on booze, but what the hell if it gives the old muscles a break. Not all flights, or flight attendants, were so relaxed. I remember coming up to Glasgow on a Saturday afternoon from the Channel Islands on the day before a Rangers v Celtic game. The plane was busy with guys going to the match and we were hardly in the air before the greens and blues were needling each other, drinking, and more dangerously smoking. It was getting out of hand until a couple of experienced Glasgow stewardesses restored order. On arrival in Scotland the plane was met by a posse of boys in blue and the errant passengers headed for a night in the cells rather than Hampden.

Most shuttle flights ended with happier memories. Latterly on the flight home to Scotland, dinner was excellent. The regulars usually left a car at Abbotsinch, so the complimentary miniatures of top-class spirits were accepted with enthusiasm but slipped into the jacket pocket rather than quaffed. One regular flier confided to me that at Hogmanay the drams he handed round so freely came from decanters filled with BA miniatures and stored for the big day. But the clock was ticking on what, in retrospect, was a golden age of inter-city travel.

14

Wars of China Teacups, Prime Steaks and Cut Prices

At the launch of the shuttle, back in the seventies, BEA had all the main route licences and the introduction of such an innovative service from Glasgow strengthened their dominance. Though it was not long before the cracks began to show. Early plans to expand the shuttle concept to Europe failed because of difficulties with the unions and resistance from foreign airlines, particularly that pesky Air France who had much to lose on the short London-Paris route. Fast trains to Manchester and London did not help, nor did the devaluation of sterling and the volatility of the oil market. And back of the envelope calculations that included all the transport times of out-of-town airports to the central business districts in big cities became something of a pastime for some of the national airline's passengers. The point-to-point times by air didn't look too good to a lot of people. Add in the fact that many of the regulars always harboured the notion that when timetables were disrupted by weather or mechanical problems elsewhere in British skies, it was always the Scots who took the brunt of the delays and it didn't look too good for travel by air on many routes. That chip on the shoulder is not a complete myth.

A taxi from the leafy suburbs to Central Station in Glasgow and a few drinks, a few more in the bar of the London "Starlight Express", as midnight neared and Motherwell slipped into the distance, followed by a comfy night in a first-class sleeper, looked tempting as opposed to flying. This train which left Glasgow Central at around 11pm and deposited you in the capital around breakfast time, ready for a day of meetings or interviews, had its attractions. But going down one night and back the next was time consuming and tiring despite the relative comfort of the sleeping compartment.

On the face of it the replacement of this routine of taxi to the airport and an hour's flight on the *Vanguard* was in some respects an improvement. But it had to be said that the flight, especially in winter, was not hugely comfortable and before the arrival of the jets many still preferred to be rocked to sleep in a cosy berth after a nightcap or six. The *Vanguard* was an interesting aircraft – the very best of passenger air transport in Britain before the introduction of jet power. I remember TV ads for the *Comet* (which after a disastrous series of deadly crashes, caused by metal fatigue, went on to a steady career as a passenger carrier and conversion to a military version, the *Nimrod*, which gave the RAF many years of good service as a sub-hunter) which showed a coin placed upright on a dining tray stay in position as you headed south smoothly at around 500 mph. This was not imaginable in the *Vanguards* which had a cavernous cabin, for the day, but tended to vibrate like a fairground ride, the whine of the turbo-prop engines making it difficult to talk to a companion. Quiet and smooth were not adjectives you could use to describe a flight in this aircraft. The *Vanguard* was an unlucky design in that the true jet, as opposed to the turbo jet, came on the scene just as it went into service. Fewer than fifty were built, mostly sold to BEA, and for years they were a familiar sight at continental and British Airports. Air Canada and Trans-Canada also bought versions. The *Vanguard* continued to fly into the 1990s and were mostly converted to freighters where vibration and noise were not an issue.

BEA was increasingly facing competition from a bunch of airlines for the domestic profit. It was a great time for aviation anoraks (Who, moi?) with many different airlines and aircraft flying out of Glasgow and Edinburgh, among them British Midland, British Eagle, BUA, and Dan Air. Aircraft used included the *Viscount*, the *Vanguard*, the *DC9*, even the *Comet* in its phoenix-like reinvention after the early in-flight disasters, and the *Bristol Britannia* known as "The Whispering Giant".

Flying in the final versions of the *Comet* (renamed the *Nimrod*, largely based on the civilian version served the RAF well on duties as a sub-hunter and maritime patrol aircraft) was a pleasant enough experience. And passengers could enjoy the antics of fellow passengers who, influenced by BEA advertising, could be seen enjoying a strange ritual. The ads made much of the smooth flight of the jet experience. As mentioned, the *Comet* was shown in-flight with passengers placing up ended coins on the food and drinks tray and the coin staying upright as the plane proceeded smoothly to London. Glaswegians, being Glaswegian, couldn't resist trying this out for themselves. Mostly the coins stayed upright, though not in a windy descent to Glasgow.

The *Britannia* was the pride of Harold Bamberg's British Eagle operation which lasted from 1948 to liquidation in 1968, though much of that time was spent in conflict with the licensing authorities and rival airlines. British Eagle also owned a couple of converted World War Two *Lancaster* bombers used for photographic surveys and spares. As happened before the war, railway companies, bus companies and shipping lines operated on the "if you can't beat them, join them" philosophy and British Eagle had for a time a joint operation with Cunard. It seems odd in retrospect that most of those alliances did not stick. The "Whispering Giant" was well named. One of the largest airliners of its time it got its nickname from the lack of over-the-ground noise produced by turbo props in the years just before the arrival of the pure jet. The *Britannia* had some technical links with the *Brabazon,* as mentioned earlier. Another link was that the *Britannia* test flying was undertaken by the legendary Bill Pegg who also flew the "Brab". The testing was not without incident and on one early flight, engine fires in the air ended with a forced landing on mudflats in Gloucestershire near Filton, the home base. No one was killed. Just another day for Bill, who said his philosophy as a test pilot was to fly the cockpit and hope the rest of the plane followed him.

The Glasgow to London air wars often hinged on other matters than the type of aircraft used and travel times. As mentioned, at the start of the shuttle in-cabin service was considered to BEA's advantage but with the arrival of competition, particularly from British Midland, things began to change. Even British Eagle got in with the act, reaching for the travel dollar with catering which included the use of Wedgewood china. BM was not quite so upmarket, but its meals were undoubtedly superior to that of the national carrier for a time and it built up an army of followers who appreciated its friendly approach rather than that of the monolithic offhand style of BEA and its rather dismissive cabin attendants, both male and female.

On the subject of quality of cabin service, an amusing story was told to fellow hacks by *The Herald*'s great sportswriter Ian Archer. Ian was on assignment in Argentina for the 1978 World

Cup when, as befitted an Oxford man of inquiring mind, he decided to take advantage of a day away from the "fitba" and explore upcountry. He pitched up at the airport and bought a ticket for a flight to an historic spot a few hundred miles inland. More interested as ever in literature and sport (or rather Partick Thistle) than the minutiae of aircraft recognition, he was nevertheless unimpressed with the oily exhaust-stained exterior of his plane. But he was frankly astounded by the superb standard of the catering. Again, china rather than polystyrene and silver service including roast beef cut from a trolley drawn down the aisle to your seat. Impressed, Ian remarked how splendid it all was compared with the plastic cutlery and sandwiches on flights back home, dictated by anti-hijacking concerns of the time and insisted on by the aviation regulators. Why the difference, he asked, sipping a pleasant brandy. The steward explained that this airline was not covered by the rules of the international aviation organisations. The steward further added that his airline had such a poor safety record that none of the international organisations would have them as a member. The rest of the journey was taken in a more sober attitude. Though a second offer of a brandy was not declined.

15

Hunting the Soviet Bears and Sinking the Tirpitz

The successors to the legends who flew the *Spitfires* and *Hurricanes* in the Second World War are now likely to be found strapped into the cockpits of *Eurofighter Typhoons* thundering down the runways of RAF Lossiemouth on training missions, or intercepting the giant four-engined Russian *Tupolev Tu-95 Bears* who have "accidentally" strayed into UK airspace, monitoring their movements. After one such incident, in March 2020, Air Chief Marshal Mike Wigston reportedly said: "These Russian bombers do not comply with international air traffic rules, are a hazard to airliners and are not welcome in our airspace. RAF *Typhoons*, alongside our NATO allies ensured these Russian aircraft posed no hazard." Given the longevity of the *Bears* – the first models were built in the fifties and the design has a planned life of another twenty years – we can expect more of such incidents in the future and the *Tupolevs* will be seen off by the *Typhoons*. "Lossie" as it is known, is one of the largest and busiest of the RAF's fast jet stations and since the operational closure of Leuchars, a few miles further down the east coast, is the only active RAF base in Scotland. It has already had recent heavy investment spent on it for the arrival of the new *Poseidon Boeing P-8* aircraft, a version of the ubiquitous *737* intended for anti-submarine patrols and to identify shipping incursions.

The Lossiemouth that will be home to the *Poseidon*s is a very different place from the founding of the base. In 1938 the government acquired a huge site, 540 acres, of agricultural land, clearing it of vegetation and farm buildings. The following years the first planes arrived, and the station formally opened. Initially a flying school was set up and thirteen *Airspeed Oxford* and five *Hawker Harts* were dumped down, parked in the open before hangars were erected. Within five months of opening, three air force men died in a mid-air collision between two *Oxfords*. The growing shadow of the war increased the pace of construction and the utilisation of Lossiemouth. And when hostilities were officially declared, a detachment of the Seaforth Highlanders joined the airmen to safeguard the station. The airspace was getting busier and busier with the arrival of more *Oxfords*, *Harts* and the North American *Harvard* plus *Fairey Battles*.

Then came the big boys – twelve *Vickers Wellingtons* flew in and saw action before the end of 1939 when they scrambled to attack the Nazi cruiser *Deutschland,* which lurked menacingly around Iceland and the Shetlands. The mission was a failure and the German warship survived the conflict and was not finally sunk until after the war when it was used as a target in bombing training missions. *Handley Page Hampdens* also went on the offensive patrolling the North Sea from "Lossie" at the start of the war. But the vile January weather put a temporary stop to these missions. The same spring Lossiemouth lost its first planes in action when three *Bristol Blenheims* were shot down over Norway.

At the time the base was among the busiest in Europe with hundreds of mechanics and radio experts under enormous pressure to keep the planes flying. That the pressure was real is emphasised by a tale once told to me by a mechanic who served there. The huge piston engines of some planes could be misfiring because of a duff spark plug. Faced with the time-tight job of spannering out plugs one by one to identify the one that was causing the trouble, the men in the oily overalls took the painful way out by lightly touching and speedily withdrawing a damp finger to spot the offender. Not something you would consider even on a humble car engine. The maintenance issue is highlighted by the fact that many planes had to be stored in fields at "Bogs of Mayne" a few miles away, also known as the satellite station RAF Elgin. This base became handy when *Hurricanes* were based there to protect the main airport from the Luftwaffe. However, in the autumn of 1940 three German *Heinkels* swooped out of the clouds to launch an attack that destroyed several RAF planes, including a *Hurricane* and a *Tiger Moth*, which presumably was left behind when the pilot training units were moved to England as preparation for the war. One of the attacking planes crashed onto the airfield and the crew of four lie buried in a local churchyard.

In the immediate years after the start of the war "Lossie" was handicapped by the stormy winters and at one stage the runways were so muddy that the *Wellingtons* based there were temporarily transferred to Lackenhurst in the gentler climate of Sussex. The failed attempts to sink the *Deutschland* were followed a few years later by attacks on the German battleship *Tirpitz*, something of a propaganda flagship of the Nazi navy. This infamous warship was operating in and around the Norwegian fjords in 1942 and Lossiemouth was the ideal base from which to mount attacks. The British government thought

BEARDMORE'S AIRSHIP FACTORY

Top left: William Beardmore & Company's Airship Factory's new construction shed in Inchinnan, finished in 1916 using over 2,300 tons of steel to complete. It would take a team of manual workers to open and close the doors, bringing in the parts of the new *R-27* airship being built there. *Right:* The hull of the *R-27*. *Bottom left:* The gondola was added and the R-27 completed after many delays in 1918.

THE DAKOTA

A British European Airways *Douglas DC3* aka the 'Dakota', with innovative wings that could withstand more than a ton of ice and served in Scotland until 1962.

CONCORDE AIRCRAFT PROTOTYPE 2

CONCORDE AIRCRAFT PROTOTYPE 2
A British Aircraft Corporation, *Bristol Brabazon*
hangar, February 1967. The first UK-built
Concorde made its maiden voyage, piloted by
Brian Trubshaw, from Filton to RAF Fairford on
April 9, 1969.

BRITISH AIRWAYS AD CAMPAIGN
A 1950s British Airways magazine advert for the
Douglas DC-7, offering fast transatlantic travel
with luxury dining options and impeccable on-
board service.

LANARK, 1910
A postcard featuring Gustav Blondeau, a French aviation pioneer, flying a biplane
whilst being watched by some of the 215,000 people who attended the first
Scottish International Aviation meeting held over eight days at Lanark, Scotland,
circa August 1910.

ERIC 'WINKLE' BROWN
Eric 'Winkle' Brown, who holds the world record for 487 test flights, preparing to take a *Sea Vampire* to *HMS Ocean* on December 3, 1945, becoming the first pilot to land on and take off from an aircraft carrier in a jet aircraft.

SEA VAMPIRE TO HMS OCEAN
The first British jet fighter powered by a single engine, the de Havilland Vampire.

LORD KELVIN
Famous for his work in mathematics and physics, Lord Kelvin, who despite refusing an invitation to join the Aeronautical Society in Glasgow University, still gave his engineering students (including Percy Pilcher) room to further their experiments.

FROM AUSTRALIA TO ENGLAND IN 8 DAYS, 20 HOURS AND 19 MINUTES
Jim Mollison, a Glaswegian who joined the RAF at eighteen and went on to find aviation fame with wife Amy Johnson as 'The Flying Sweethearts'. Mollison's plane arrives in England after a record-breaking flight from Australia which took 8 days, 20 hours and 19 minutes.

RENFREW AIRPORT

A *British Eagle* leaving behind Renfrew Airport's distinctive parabola arch and viewing terrace.

END OF AN ERA

Featured in the novel *Return to the Lost Planet* by Angus MacVicar, the airport was decommissioned in 1966, handling 1.4 million passengers in its final year (over ten times the amount of passengers compared to the first year of operations).

GLASGOW AIRPORT

Staff and visitors line up to see the Queen open Glasgow Airport (originally named 'Abbotsinch') on June 27, 1966.

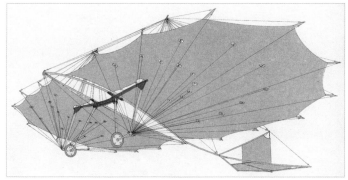

THE HAWK
The design of Percy Pilcher's 'Hawk' hang glider, 1890.

THE 'GLIDING' MACHINE
Dorothy and Percy Pilcher testing their wood and canvas experiment, the *Hawk*, in Eynsford, 1898.

READY TO START   IN MID-AIR

THE FATAL ACCIDENT TO MR. PILCHER: THE "GLIDING" MACHINE AT WORK

FATAL ACCIDENT
The Graphic newspaper reporting Pilchers hang gliding accident, sadly resulting in his death in 1899.

VC10

The Vickers' *VC10* nearing completion in February 2, 1962 – the biggest jet airliner ever built in Europe – went on to achieve the fastest crossing of the Atlantic by a subsonic jet airliner in 5 hours and 1 minute, a record that was held for forty-one years, until February 2020.

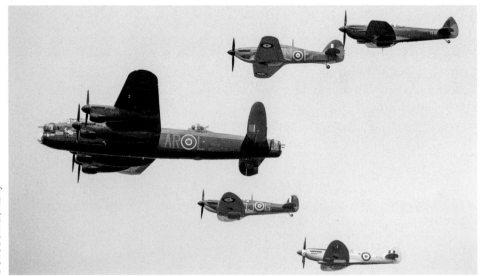

THE BATTLE OF BRITAIN MEMORIAL FLIGHT

On the final day of the Royal International Air Tattoo in 2017 at Fairford, The Battle of Britain Memorial Flight includes a *Lancaster* bomber, a *Hurricane* and three *Spitfires*.

THE DE HAVILLAND COMET

Staff and crew wave goodbye to the de Havilland *Comet*, the world's first commercial jetliner, leaving Heathrow for Johannesburg, May 2, 1952.

THE SUNDERLAND FLYING BOAT

One of the most widely used flying boats of WW2, and made to British Air Ministry regulation for service with the RAF, a *Short Sunderland* takes to the air.

THE VISCOUNT

The *Vickers Viscount* entered service in 1953 and by mid-1958, the BEA's fleet of the aircraft had taken 2.75 million passengers around the world in over 200,000 flight hours.

THE VANGUARD

The successor to the *Viscount*, another Vickers aircraft, the *Vanguard*, which despite being ideal for shuttle routes, was noted for a great deal of vibration and inside cabin noise.

BARRA AIRPORT

From a sandy beach at Barra Airport, passengers board a *Loganair Twin Otter*, which was also used in conjunction with Scottish Ambulance Service (SAS) to provide air ambulance capability in 2020.

© imageBROKER / Alamy

GLASGOW AIRPORT FROM ABOVE

A drone captures the bird's eye view of the runways of Glasgow Airport. Carrying over 9 million passengers per year, it has been in operation since 1933, when it was in use as a facility for (among other planes) the RAF's *Wapiti IIA* aircraft.

© ALAN OLIVER / Alamy

EDINBURGH AIRPORT FROM ABOVE

An aerial drone view of Edinburgh Airport which, with only one runway and terminal, is the sixth-busiest airport in the United Kingdom.

© Paul White – Transport Infrastructures / Alamy

an important boost to public spirit would be achieved if she could be sunk. The importance of destroying a ship that was an icon in Germany was demonstrated by the strength of the attack from Lossiemouth – more than twenty planes took part in a series of raids on the warship. *Lancaster*s, *Halifaxe*s and *Short Stirling*s were all involved; still the warship survived various assaults in bad weather. But the RAF is nothing if not determined. And a couple of years later the *Tirpitz* was finally despatched to the deep in the autumn and winter of 1944. A series of attacks, this time even stronger in numbers of aircraft, completed the job. Thirty-eight *Lancaster*s flew out of Lossiemouth, Kinloss and Milltown, a small satellite field in the area, and dropped twelve-thousand-pound "Tallboy" bombs (designed by Barnes Wallis of Dambusters fame) that destroyed the vessel and gave Britain a propaganda victory that it had longed for for years. Sadly, the years between the two *Tirpitz* attacks had been marked by numerous fatal accidents in training exercises and again the weather up in the north east was partly to blame along with aircraft that were perhaps over utilised by the pressures of war and inexperienced fliers.

However, the famous muddy runaways were a thing of the past as an engineering battalion of the US Army Air Force had surfaced the runways enabling *Wellington*s to take part in massive raids on Germany with up to 1,000 bombers per raid being assembled from several bases in Britain. The use of some aircraft intended for training purposes was required to meet the numbers of bombers required.

Like Machrihanish, far to the south and west, Lossiemouth had strong associations with the Fleet Air Arm. The RAF light blue gave way to the dark blue of the Royal Navy when in 1946 "Lossie" became HMS Fulmar. Milltown became HMS Fulmar II. Carrier pilots on completion of training could land on *HMS*

Theseus ploughing around the nearby Moray Firth. It was nerve-racking work especially in bad weather with the deck pitching unpredictably around in a way that a surface land runway never, ever, did. An HMS Fulmar II colleague told me that you did not know fear until you had looked down from a couple of thousand feet at a carrier, a mile or so ahead of you, battling its way through spray and white horses and realising that this tiny speck on the ocean was where you had to land. Another ex-Fleet Arm man, by now a lawyer, told me that on occasion he had a half bottle of brandy as company in his *Fairey Swordfish* cockpit in the war. I found it ironic that in peacetime he came to be the scourge of the drink driver. "Ah," he whispered to me, "I never knew then if I was coming back!".

In its days as HMS Fulmar, Lossiemouth saw a lot of the *Buccaneer* jet which could deliver nuclear weapons. The North Sea was a playground for these fast planes and in the days before Britain was reduced to a couple of carriers, *HMS Victorious, HMS Hermes, HMS Ark Royal and HMS Eagle* took part in exercises involving *Buccaneers*. But perhaps the most memorable escapade in the life of this fine aircraft came in 1967 and it was not a military event. That spring the giant oil tanker *Torrey Canyon* was adrift off Cornwall spewing out oil that was threatening an environmental disaster. The solution: bomb the tanker and set the oil ablaze before it could do too much harm. A great chance for the *Buccaneer* pilots to have a spot of target practice and do the beaches and wildlife a favour. They jumped at the chance and succeeded in clearing up the mess.

The Fleet Air Arm era ended in 1972 when the station (the legendary Eric "Winkle" Brown, featured elsewhere in this book, was Station Commander at the time) was returned to RAF control. A helicopter search and rescue unit was set up, much later to be removed, and crews trained on a new fast jet, the

Jaguar. But Lossiemouth had not seen the last of the *Buccaneer*. In the 1980s it returned as an RAF maritime strike squadron. Other aircraft used in the base's new role included the *Shackleton* and another fast jet fighter, the *Hawker Hunter*. And when the Buccaneer finally retired it was replaced by *Tornados*. At the turn of the century Lossiemouth was the RAF's busiest fast jet station.

But it was soon to be faced with the threat of closure. In 2005 the Ministry of Defence had announced it was to be the main base for operating Lockheed Martin's *F-35 Lightning*, a multi-role stealth combat aircraft. In volume terms this is a remarkable plane with around 550 built by 2020. But there were dark clouds ahead. A defence review raised doubts about whether this remarkable aircraft would ever settle in Scotland and the very survival of the base was in doubt. So important is the base to employment in the local area that in November 2010, a march demanding the threat to close the base was lifted attracted around 7,000 people and gained the support of prominent local and national politicians. As the history of aviation shows, reviews and counter reviews seem addictive both in the military and commercial sectors. So, in the July of the next year the Ministry of Defence did a U-turn as dramatic as that of a jet fighter and the base was saved, though the *F35* was to operate from an airfield in England. Apart from the decision to save the base there was an announcement of serious spending on infrastructure including a new taxiway, bomb-proof shelters for aircraft and a new headquarters unit. All good news. But as in the music business, where you are only as good as your last hit, in aviation you are only as safe as your last defence review. Governments seem to be as addicted as much to U-turns as air show stunt pilots are to be looping the loop.

Not far down the east coast from Lossiemouth is Leuchars, near a long flat sandy bay at St Andrews. The sands are a playground for tourists to the home of golf and an attraction made famous in the film *Chariots of Fire*. The area was not new to aerial activity – in the early years of the last century sightseers could have watched the "stringbags" of the recently formed Royal Flying corps sweep down from the clouds to land alongside the world's most famous golf course. These early military aviators favoured St Andrews as a refuelling spot thanks to the many garages catering for early touring motorists. Leuchars is one of the oldest military flying bases in the world. As far back as 1908 the area was flirting with aviation. The Army used the area as a test base for experiments with man-lifting kites and the Royal Engineers had set up a training camp in Tentsmuir forest for the balloonists used by the Army as "spies in the sky" to plot enemy movements on the ground in warfare. It was during the First World War in 1916, that workers began levelling a site on a local farm as a proper airbase and work was still going on in 1918 when the armistice was signed. Leuchars formally became an RAF base in 1920, mainly as a training unit and was used by the Navy for carrier training, like that provided later by Lossiemouth. The good citizens of St Andrews itself were, even then, making the most of the fame of the golf course to maximise the tourist dollar and the idea of getting the wealthy to fly into the new air base was attractive, but ahead of its time. Interestingly, around 100 years later at Machrihanish, when a new course called The Dunes and a holiday village was constructed near the long established Machrihanish links, one of the attractions was that the airport was only a few hundred yards away from the runway where you could land a private jet.

St Andrews' connection with aviation was still strong in the 1930s when it was a popular destination for the flying circuses touring the country, selling joyrides and showing off the aerobatic abilities of the planes of the day. But as the clouds of war darkened, RAF Leuchars was given more of an operational than a training role. Earlier in this book the arguments about who achieved the first kill in an air battle over the Firth of Forth were mentioned. Leuchars had its own claim to fame. On September 4, 1939, a *Lockheed Hudson* from the base attacked a *Dornier 18* over the North Sea. The result of this mission was "inconclusive", but the *Hudson* was said to be the first British aircraft to engage the enemy in the Second World War.

Another *Hudson* was involved in a more successful operation the next year when it found a German prison ship, the *Altmark*, and aided a Navy warship to intercept it and free more than 200 Brits who were held on board. Maritime patrol was basically the role played by aircraft flying out of Leuchars. Though it had an unusual wartime use for a spell when BOAC, formed at the start of the war by the amalgamation of Imperial Airway and British Airways, ran a route from Scotland to Stockholm. BOAC also operated a civilian registered *Mosquito* on the route when Swedish ball-bearings were vital to the wartime industry. The base also launched rescue missions to return personnel who had crash-landed or been diverted to Sweden.

In the years following the war the Fife airfield passed from Coastal Command – with its emphasis on anti-submarine work to Fighter Command and then the sportsmen and women still drawn to the home of golf found the skies above them a tad noisier – the jets had arrived, much more disconcerting than the old *Tiger Moth* of the St Andrews University Air Squadron. The *Gloster Meteor* was the first of many fast jets to become a familiar sight in the area. Soon also to be seen were the *English Electric Lightening*, and the *McDonnell Douglas Phantoms* (to be replaced eventually by the *Tornado F.3*). Even the University had upgraded to a training *Chipmunk*. But the glory days which included an addition to maritime patrol work, a spell hosting the RAF mountain rescue unit, air interception work at the height of the cold war and a helicopter search and rescue unit were over. That MOD predilection to have a review at the drop of a hat meant that this historic air base was doomed. The site was transferred to Army control in 2014. So, an air adventure that has started with manned balloons and moved through hot and cold wars, from biplanes to jets, was finally history. But at least the golfers found the skies did not provide a noisy distraction as they crouched over a dangerously long putt.

An interesting coda to the story of the RAF in Scotland, particularly in the northeast is the epic tale of *MacRobert's Reply*, and a family's remarkable philanthropy. Many know the name and the story, but not much of the family and its charitable legacy. Lady Rachel MacRobert was American born, the daughter of parents who were mountaineers, famous explorers and authors. Her husband Sir Alex was of fairly humble Scottish extraction who had made a fortune in India. They had three sons – Alasdair, Roderic, and Iain. Alasdair was killed aged just twenty-six in a civil flying accident. The baronial title was passed to Roderic who was a pilot in the RAF. Roderic flew *Hurricanes* and died in one while leading an attack on a German-held airfield. He was also just twenty-six . The baronetcy passed to Iain who was a pilot officer in the RAF, having joined straight out of Cambridge. Against all the odds the MacRoberts suffered a third tragedy in a row when six weeks after Roderic's death, Iain's *Blenheim* failed to return from a search and rescue mission from Sullom Voe in the Shetlands. His body was never found. He was only twenty-four years old.

The response of Rachel MacRobert to these three tragedies was remarkable: she made a gift of £25,000 to the RAF and asked them to use it to buy a bomber to be called "MacRobert's Reply". A *Short Stirling* bomber handed over to the RAF late in 1941 was duly given Rachel's chosen name. It took part in twelve missions. But it was damaged in a collision with a *Spitfire* at Peterhead airbase and replaced by another *Stirling* which carried the name. This plane was shot down and lost in a minelaying raid in 1942. After her original donation Rachel MacRobert gifted a further £20,000 to help buy four *Hurricanes* to aid the RAF in the Middle East. Three were named after her sons and the fourth was given her own name.

The RAF revived the tradition in 1982 when a *Buccaneer* was given the name and the family crest painted on the fuselage beneath the cockpit. Several other fast jets carried the name until finally, in October 2018, when the last plane to be called "MacRobert's Reply", a *Tornado*, was scrapped. Between 1943 and 1950 Lady MacRobert founded a series of charity trusts to "provide the means and organisation to foster in young people the best traditional ideals and spirit" which she believed had prompted so many young people, including her own sons, to fight in the Second World War. The MacRobert family will never be forgotten.

16

Flying with the Birds and Jumping Out of Planes

Not all the flying to be seen in the Scottish skies uses engine power. I may be a confirmed Argyll man, but I also enjoy an occasional inland jaunt to the southern shores of Loch Leven and a visit to the famous RSPB bird sanctuary where the range of feathered fliers to be seen is remarkable. Ospreys, lapwings, and at times congregations of many thousands of pink footed geese and other breeds are on show. The birds often compete for air space with other soundless fliers – gliders from the little Portmoak airfield at nearby Scotlandwell. A hike around the bird sanctuary's nature trails is a delight under the blue skies of a summer day. Lift your eyes upwards from the loch and the footpaths and you are almost certain to see a couple or so gliders serenely drifting around in total silence on the hot air bouncing off the Lomond hills that surround the water. It is a pleasant sight that has delighted visitors and locals for years.

Gliding is a more popular hobby in Scotland than most people appreciate, with the Scottish Gliding Association listing around ten active or defunct clubs. Portmoak is the HQ of the Association and is the most active gliding site in the country. The safety record of gliding is impressive and there is no need to worry about these engineless machines drifting into the path of a jet, military or commercial, since the Association has written agreements with National Air Traffic on procedures for entering controlled airspace. If you want to learn to fly on the wind after being hauled aloft by a tug this is the place to learn, though there are clubs, in among other places, the Cairngorms, Deeside and the Highlands. The glider enthusiasts using Portmoak for a large part spend their time in lazy circles around the Bishop Hill area of the Lomonds. But it would be a mistake to think that wind power can only take you a handful of miles or so, or keep you safely aloft for twenty minutes.

Back in 1971 John Williams, of Scotlandwell, took off from Portmoak in his *Antares* glider at around seven in the morning and stayed aloft for almost twelve hours, travelling across Scotland at least twice. He was able to do this because of exceptional weather. In certain conditions northwest winds blowing across the Highlands set up a ripple of air currents that can be surfed by a skilled glider pilot. Scotland has more days like this than many European countries and is something of a mecca for enthusiasts. Another mecca, this time more for light aircraft fanatics, is a short hop away from Loch Leven: Scone.

Close to Perth, this is not the sort of airfield you are likely to see an *Airbus* or *Boeing* – unless it is a vapour trail in the sky. But this attractive little airport just might have been where the pilot of that flash of silver hurtling west out over the Atlantic may well have learned to fly, or at least caught the piloting bug. A hub of private aviation down the years, Scone has had a famed flying academy. One of many celebrities who learned to fly here was Jimmy Logan, the much-loved Scottish comedian, a natural successor in comedy to Harry Lauder and a thoroughly nice man. Logan, also a brilliant straight actor, was not the most likely of private pilots.

In his autobiography *It's a Funny Life*, published in 1998, he admits to never giving a thought to piloting his own plane until the late 1950s when he was getting to the peak of his career making big money from radio, television, comedy, films and pantomimes. The pantos alone brought home £500 a week, a huge sum these days. He had a Rolls Royce – registration number JL10 – a ten room house in Glasgow's affluent West End and was living the life of a star. But he had never thought of the private plane bit until a wealthy friend asked if he wanted to learn to fly. Jimmy wasn't particularly keen. He was too busy with the theatre. But his pal persisted, and Jimmy found himself driving up to what he called "a big green field" in Perthshire.

He climbed into a little *Chipmunk* and took one look at the dials in front of him thinking "I'll never learn this in a million years". But after that first little lesson was over, he was hooked. Flying can indeed be an addiction. Jimmy's instructor was a remarkable figure around what was known then as "Scone Aerodrome", to use a term that has fallen out of fashion. Tom Blyth had flown bombers in the Second World War and had earned the Air Force Cross and the Distinguished Flying Cross. In his book, Jimmy recalled that before they climbed into the cockpit Tom conducted what he called "brief flights checks", which the star remarked appeared to consist of checking they had two wings, a rudder at the back and two wheels on the bottom. Then it was up and away, and Jimmy was hooked. He bought a four-seater *Miles Gemini* with the call sign "Golf, Alpha, Juliet, Whisky, Charlie". Jimmy, who enjoyed a social dram on occasion, was amused to be flying around in a craft called "Whisky Charlie" – apt for a Scottish comedian. Years of fun and adventures followed. Telling of those happy days Jimmy was modest about his ability, but he was the sort of guy who liked to get things right, be it a comedy skit or flying himself around the British Isles. Though he does recount a particularly bumpy landing which prompted one of the airport ground staff to congratulate him on "landing at 1.20, 1.21, 1.22, and 1.24"!

It was all a long way from his days in the Logan Family shows in the old Metropole theatre in Stockwell Street in Glasgow. Jimmy was reminded not to get carried away when he took his elderly mother for a sightseeing trip over the Kintyre peninsula. Pointing out the sights his mother, a typical Glaswegian, intervened: "Keep quiet, mind where you're going". But there's no doubt the passenger, herself once a star on the halls, was proud of the pilot. Jimmy loved that little plane.

Another Glasgow celebrity, boxing promoter and manager Tommy Gilmour, told me a tale for use in the book, *A Boxing Dynasty*, that we co-authored, which painted a picture of private flying after the Second World War. Tommy's dad was also a successful man in the boxing business and liked to make regular visits to Glasgow's favourite holiday spot before the cheap charter flights to such as the Costa del Sol took over . . . the Isle of Man. Being a man of means, when he went over there by steamer each summer, he booked a cabin for the family. One year he left it too late in making a booking. But a pal pointed out that he knew someone who frequented Ayr racecourse who had a private plane. Problem solved – this guy would fly the family out to the island. The annual break was back on. The chap who came up with this idea did issue a veiled warning; remarking that the pilot liked a dram or four and it would be better not to pay him until they were safely on the ground in the IOM.

Young Tommy, excitedly looking forward to his holiday, turned up at the airport to be met by a character looking like a First World War flying ace, fresh from central casting. The pilot wore a leather helmet and sported a silk scarf and goggles. He calmly ushered them on board, and they did make it to the island, but the flight was not without incident. At one point the cabin door vibrated open and the Gilmour family got a good clear view of the Irish Sea a few hundred feet below them. The Biggles style character at the controls took it calmly and asked young Tommy's uncle Bob, the nearest passenger, to lean out, catch it and close it. Which Uncle Bob did with sangfroid to match the pilot. Tommy also recalled with a grin that as the destination neared and the fuel load lessened, the pilot shuffled them around like chess pieces to balance the plane for landing! Not like the private jet, of today.

Scone, of course, is not alone as a flying academy. Prestwick even when busy with commercial and freight aircraft was a base for training pilots for major airlines. Golfers on the famed links of Ayrshire were used to jets doing almost constant training flights overhead and the sight of small training aircraft pottering about above the lush greens and fairway. One pilot who learned his flying here was a young man from my local village of Eaglesham in Renfrewshire, a short hop from Prestwick itself. Andrew Gordon went on to be a BA captain flying *Boeing 777*s to the States and Africa. Over a coffee he told me of his time at the BA training school:

Courses were made up of sixteen cadets, normally from various backgrounds. My lot consisted mainly of university graduates, but we also had a submariner, one guy who was ex-Navy and a couple of school leavers! For me, it was a little bit like returning to university, but with a large flying school attached. As well as the flying, there was a lot of bookwork and studying involved, but all of us were there for one thing – to graduate as airline pilots. There was mixed previous flying experience amongst us, from none, right up to one cadet who had previous experience as an instructor. He was the first to take the initial general flying test and set a suitable standard, as when he returned to the crew room, he informed us all that he had failed. This did have us wondering about the standard you had to achieve, but as we all steadily passed this first test, he did become the butt of one or two jokes. (He did go on to graduate and gain his wings, though.)

As you gained experience, so the flying became more varied. Solo cross-country flights were always good fun. Having planned your route and received approval from your instructor, off you went. One day whilst navigating back to Prestwick, we had a cadet who made a radio call to Scottish Air Traffic Control, pretending to be uncertain of his position (something which you do during your training). He was duly informed he was just north-west of Dumfries – having missed Prestwick by approximately thirty miles. It is said Air Traffic Control soon became wise to cadets "pretending", so when they had anyone from the college calling up saying this, the first question they asked was, "Where do you think you are?"

Andrew illustrated the thoroughness of the training and importance placed, from the start, on the understanding that the pilot must always expect the unexpected:

The latter stages of your flying training were on the twin-engine *Seneca*. During this training, engine failures were practised. The instructor would slowly close one of the throttles so the engine on that side was only at idle. This would cause the aircraft to yaw. To stop this, you push the rudder pedal corresponding to the side on which the engine is still operating. The other leg is now doing nothing on the side on which the engine had failed. This was trained as dead leg (doing nothing) dead engine. The story goes that when this happened to one of the students, having controlled the aircraft, he proceeded to say "Left leg dead. No! Right leg dead. No!" at which point the instructor intervened and shouted, "We're all dead!" Once you had successfully passed all your flying tests, if you had any hours left (there was a requirement to complete 200 flying hours) you could take an aircraft to effectively "burn" hours. I managed a Scottish cross-country trip, flying along the west coast, across to Aberdeen and back to Prestwick. This left me an hour or so. I duly arranged to take a *Seneca* for a short flight. A quick phone call to my Gran in East Kilbride and off I went. Arriving over her house, there she was with my Grandpa, in the back garden – complete with a waving white sheet! A few turns overhead and off back to Prestwick I went.

On returning, I was invited into the Chief Instructor's office. They had received a phone call from a resident complaining that an aircraft from the college was doing aerobatics over East Kilbride and as I was the only one there? I duly explained that it was in a *Seneca* (which is not aerobatic) and therefore it could not have been me. Although I may have done a few steep turns. Suitably reminded of the professional standards expected, off I went with tail between legs. Despite these, which on reflection are light-hearted stories, the fifteen months at the college were intense. Although you achieved 200 hours flying, most of your time was spent in the classroom, revising for the eighteen written exams which were taken at the end of the course. We all worked hard and enjoyed our time there, graduating successfully.

A nice tribute to good schooling from a flyer who had to deal with an emergency or two when he finally achieved that dream of sitting in the left-hand seat of a big jet and successfully transporting a few hundred businessmen and families across the continents and oceans.

I don't think young Andrew had the occasion to use a parachute in his airline life. But that busy little airfield at Scone was used at times by amateur skydivers seeking a dose of adrenalin. Sometimes such jumps were taken by the less-than-expert who had been sponsored by friends and employers to raise money for charity. When Harry Reid, who went on to be a distinguished editor of *The Herald*, was in his early days at *The Scotsman* (or "Scotsperson" as female journalists would have it) he took the notion to organise a charity jump with other scribes on the paper. The idea was enthusiastically endorsed and the jump at Scone arranged. The upside was the cash raised for a good cause, the downside that the douce Edinburgh folk nearly didn't get their paper the next day. A surplus of sprained ankles and bruised bodies meant the staff was so depleted that it was a struggle to fill the pages of that august publication.

Scone is often referred to as Perth's airport, a natural consequence of its proximity to the city. These days it is a hub for one of my favourite charities SCAA (Scotland's Charity Air Ambulance) which has the fine postal address: The Control Tower, Perth Airport, Scone, Perthshire, PH2 6PL, should you want to send a donation. It has a couple of choppers especially designed for air ambulance work, one based in Perth and the other in Aberdeen. Its lifesaving work is done in conjunction with the Scottish Ambulance Service, two government funded helicopters and two fixed wing aircraft which are tasked through the 999 emergency service. A recent development is a clinical training unit in a hangar at Perth, where trainers work surrounded by reminders of the history of a base that, in its publicity material, the SCAA still calls Scone Aerodrome. The service costs around four million a year to run and in 2019, before the arrival of the second helicopter at Aberdeen, it increased the number of call-outs from 105 to 154. Nearly a third of the incidents attended were road traffic accidents and most of the others involved heart or stroke emergences. Work well worth supporting.

17

The Name of the Game: Survival. The Winner: Loganair

If you have reached this chapter in this book, you will have realised by now that it is not too hard to start an airline. You lease or buy a few planes and find a few optimistic fellow enthusiasts with a bob or two sloshing around in the bank – or even better get a bank itself to back you – and then you look around for somewhere you think is desperate to support an air service. Some good recruitment advertising, an attractive logo, and an eye-catching paint job on the planes, plus recruiting the right chief pilot and you are off. That is the easy bit. The hard bit is to survive. No one in Scotland knows more about this than Scott Grier. That is why he aptly titled his history of Loganair's first fifty years (from 1962–2012) *A Scottish Survivor*. When running an airline, survival is the name of the game. So, the feat of making Loganair the oldest name in continuous use in aviation in the UK is something to celebrate. And this gritty little gem of an airline survived the pandemic better that most. Before setting out on the adventurous and labyrinthine story of the airline's fifty-plus years, an anecdote hints at one secret of a long life in a business littered with the headstones of company collapses.

Scott Grier may have been largely a money man and top manager in this story of a great airline survivor, but he also knew – and made sure everyone else working in the company knew – that good service was vital. There is evidence that his insistence on treating the customer correctly was ingrained in staff from receptionists, to stewards, to pilots in a story told by a globetrotting engineer friend of mine called Jimmy Turner, a weel-kent figure in Largs and on Arran. On a jaunt to one of his old haunts in South America, Jimmy told of disembarking a British Airways 747 and entering a crowded and chaotic Santiago airport arrival hall. Waiting for his luggage to come around on the carousel amid the noise and confusion he spotted a "four striper" pilot and some of his crew helping passengers with luggage and remarked that this was service above and beyond. The skipper replied that if you had learned your airline flying on Loganair it was just part of the job. Old habits die hard!

The in-depth history of Loganair is beyond the scope of this book. But even in a digest form it is a remarkable one. It was a long time before you could use the words *Boeing 747* and Loganair in the same sentence. Sadly, these days you might hear a passenger ask who the Logan of Loganair was? The answer is a man Scott Grier calls: "Surely one of Scotland's great post-war entrepreneurs, Willie Logan." Changed days, for at the start of Loganair, Willie Logan was known throughout the land and featured regularly in Scotland's newspapers, both tabloid and broadsheet. Most of the "ink" he received concerned his business adventures as an industrialist. He may have been the "Mr Big" of his construction enterprises, but he was a shrewd hands-on operator who knew better than to hide away in the head office – he travelled the country incessantly keeping tabs on major civil engineering projects. What better way to do this than by air? So, in the days before Loganair was born, he chartered flights from an air taxi firm called Capitol Services (Aero Limited) flying out mostly from the old Renfrew airport near Paisley and Turnhouse in Edinburgh.

Among several light aircraft it had was the ubiquitous twin-engined *Piper Aztec*, one of the most successful aircraft of all time. When the air-taxi firm hit financial turbulence, far from unusual in the business, Willie Logan, chairman of his own construction company also became chairman of Loganair in February 1962. The new "airline" had one plane, again a trusty *Aztec*, based at Renfrew where, under its nose, day in and day out, flew the passenger carrying workhorses of BEA which in its many guises would latterly become the major opposition to the fledgling airline. A humble start.

A legendary figure on the Scottish flying scene, Duncan McIntosh who had worked for Capitol, became chief pilot and manager. Loganair opened the throttles for lift-off. Willie Logan had joined his father's small stone-cutting business in Muir of Ord, Ross-shire in 1932. He grew it into a civil engineering giant and by 1962 he was travelling 2,000 miles a week from Muir of Ord overlooking his empire. One of his contracts involved the new Tay Road Bridge and he also built, among other projects, much of Cumbernauld. His photographs show a genial sort of chap who was really enjoying his aviation adventure. And if for weather or other reasons he was grounded, he kept a Jaguar in Dundee (near that tiny Tayside strip that is Dundee Airport) and a Rolls in Glasgow. As befits his Highland background he was a "wee free" churchman who avoided Sunday working unless it was vital. He was lucky to have as a friend and pilot Duncan

McIntosh who in his career logged around 10,000 flying hours between 1941 and 1981. McIntosh was amongst those who set up Glasgow Flying Club in the sixties. That little *Piper* must have seemed a walk in the park for a man who had flown *Spitfires* off a carrier and after the war was a test pilot on Navy jets. An indication of the fame of "Captain Mac", as he was affectionately known, is that Duncan McIntosh Road is the address of the little Cumbernauld Airport near Glasgow. (Originally a grass strip, the arrival of the new town saw it asphalted and upgraded. It is now much used for training and maintenance. It once had a little air show which featured a mock dogfight between a *Spitfire* and an *Me 109*. That must have been a fascinating sight.)

McIntosh was much influenced by the activities of Ted Fresson in opening up, pre-war, the Highlands and Islands by air. Later when BA dumped some the routes (Glasgow – Barra, Campbeltown, Islay and Tiree in 1975/76) in the west he realised the opportunity for Loganair. Loganair took over Campbeltown, Islay, Tiree, and Barra scheduled services as a result of collaboration between the Scottish Office, the CAA, BA and Loganair.

It was clear even to BA that their aircraft were unsuitable for such thin routes. The aviation industry was regulated until around 1990 and Scott Grier told me that: "For Loganair to get onto any route there had to be a Licence Hearing before the CAA almost always in London when BA instructed very expensive barristers to defend their monopoly. Our frustration was that we believed we could offer a better service especially on thin lifeline routes." It seems that to the authorities the fact that the nationalised carrier was making losses, paid for by the taxpayer, was of little importance.

So, the early days of this long-lasting airline were filled with optimism and dreams of expansion. Duncan McIntosh's optimism was generally well founded and much of the dream became reality. But sadly, Willie Logan was to die in an air crash in the winter of 1966 before the great days.

He had an appointment in Inverness and on that day his own little airline did not have a plane free and he took the decision to charter another *Piper Aztec* from the recently formed Strathair. Unfortunately, this new air service based in Auchterarder was not on a list of non-scheduled operators covered by the Logan Group insurance policy. The *Aztec* headed from Edinburgh to Inverness in December darkness and cloud, on the descent to the airport it crashed into a tree-covered hilltop and Willie Logan was killed instantly whilst the pilot survived despite severe injury. The Logan Group insurers refused to pay out as Strathair was not one of their approved operators. Strathair had only the minimum £3,500 per person passenger liability insurance required by aviation's Warsaw Convention and this meagre sum was paid to Loganair. Willie Logan's widow lost her company owned house and started legal proceedings against the Strathair pilot. It was a sad time. Willie Logan lies in a grave in Dingwall that is marked by a monument resembling part of the Tay Bridge. A proposal by the SNP that the bridge in Dundee be named "The Logan Bridge" never came to frui-tion. A shame, but the backers of the idea who got much public support and wanted the name change to perpetuate the memory of a man who was "synonymous with the character of a true Scotsman – compassionate, religious, astute, and industrious" got it right.

It was a turbulent start to a new era for Willie Logan's airline. At the controls Duncan McIntosh set about building on Fresson's ideas of bringing reliable transport to areas of Scotland isolated by their geography. Captain Mac continued to be the airline's managing director till the early eighties. His preferred area of operation was in the cockpit, rather than flying a boardroom.

He had also come through a less heavily regulated era than the current one. Scotland's wild weather seldom deterred him – nor the lack of instrumentation assistance now enjoyed by pilots and he flew on occasion in conditions that would have troubled a flier without his great skill and breadth of experience. He got the job done and undoubtedly improved life in the Highlands and Islands immensely.

Right from the start Loganair faced a perfect storm of arguments over subsidies, constantly changing air regulations, competition from national airlines and local upstarts with ambition, and the fact that transport links on the ground and on the lochs were in a vast and complex process of development. The face of Scotland was changing with the building of bridges, dual carriageways and motorways that cut road journey times. And, of course, in the north west competition from MacBraynes' ubiquitous ferries was fierce. In his history of Loganair, Scott Grier quotes the old rhyme . . .

The earth belongs unto the Lord
And all that it contains
Except the Western Isles
And they are David MacBraynes'

If ownership of the earth was clear what was the situation in the air? It was not just the Western Isles that were a problem; travel to the far north and the Orkney Islands and Shetlands was changing with improving ferry services from Aberdeen, now reached in around three hours from Glasgow by road.

From Loganair's point of view, BA's emerging activities in the area were a major problem. Loganair's frustration was that BA had been operating in the area since 1947 and were offering poor service with inappropriately sized aircraft. Despite making huge losses they refused to give up any routes. Scott Grier was told by Bob Ayling, BA's CEO in the nineties, that the airline had never made a profit on Scottish internal routes since 1947. An example of how they resisted competition is, for instance, when Loganair applied to carry passengers back from Stornoway (having delivered the newspapers), BA lodged an objection and Loganair was limited to carrying fifteen passengers a week. It was an unsettling time for airlines in Scotland and all sorts of scheduling problems arose, particularly how to handle passenger traffic arriving mid-morning in Glasgow or Edinburgh from the south and finding they were too late for a once a day flight north or west. A battle of timetables and disorganisation ensued that gave Loganair headaches. And perhaps with hindsight the idea of concentrating the growing of scheduled service was over optimistic, that greater growth might be had instead from air taxi and charter work, getting newspapers to far flung areas the same day they were printed and gaining a foothold in air ambulance work.

No matter the politics or visionary planning, it is vital for an airline to have the right aircraft for the job. In the days when Duncan McIntosh was at the controls of Loganair, in the left hand seat as he might say, the choice of planes to buy was much wider than what pertains today when the industry is dominated by *Boeing, Douglas* and *Airbus* plus a few specialists in providing craft for feeder and local services. As a flyer's flyer McIntosh had a soft spot for the *Beech 18*, an attractive aircraft which he told the press was "a real pilot's aeroplane and thoroughly rewarding to fly". To underline his affection, he called this pretty little craft, in the red and white colours of Loganair of the time, "The Queen of the skies". The love affair had come to fruition in 1968 when the company bought one. The *Beech 18* built by Beechcraft in Wichita, Kansas, was not just a pretty face. More than 9,000 had been built when production ended in 1969. It was used in 1969–70 on the company's first international scheduled service between Aberdeen and Stavanger. Incidentaly Scott Grier told me that he often reflected ruefully that Loganair, with a wonderful sense of timing discontinued the service about five minutes before oil was discovered in the North Sea. On the home front the *Beech* was ideal for lugging the increasingly heavy weight of newspaper deliveries to Stornoway from Glasgow. The one flaw in the *Beech 18* was a tendency to enjoy spells out of action in the hangar being "spannered" back into service. And its nine-passenger capacity was less than impressive. Good looks and fun to fly wasn't everything.

The *Beech* was followed by the company's largest plane to date in 1969 when a *Short Skyvan* arrived. The name said it all, this was an unattractive looking slab-sided workhorse with few pretentions of luxury. But despite its boxy look, which was actually very efficient for cargo loading – including the occasional bullock which put reality into the phrase travelling "cattle class" – its short take-off and landing ability suited Highland airports. However, it was expensive to operate and it turned out to be a costly buy. Scott Grier considered it a mistake as it never really realised the utilisation figures necessary for success. Its demise could have been predicted when it was chartered to take homing pigeons to the Faroe Islands and the birds got back to Glasgow before the plane. In the sixties and seventies Loganair used *Britten Norman Islanders* in various configures. The purchase of *BN2* with its outstanding short field performance transformed Loganair's fortunes. The ambulance work and particularly the inter-island air service in Orkney and later Shetland followed. The Orkney north isles services continues today still with the *BN2* and is almost unchanged

since 1967. In acknowledgement of the good work of air ambulance services they named a number of these aircraft after many
of the pioneers of Scottish aviation: "Sister Jean Kennedy"
(who had made more than 200 air ambulance flights before
dying in an air crash near Islay airport), "Captain E E Fresson",
"Captain David Barclay" (A BEA legend who had also flown
for Midland & Scottish Air Ferries, Northern & Scottish Airways
and Scottish Airways), "Sir James Young Simpson" (a pioneer
of anaesthesia), "Robert McKean" (Chairman of BEA Scottish
Airways and supporter of air ambulance services generally),
"E L Gander Dower" (who set up Aberdeen Airways in 1934)
and "Captain Eric Starling" (a major figure in the history of the
Scottish air ambulance service).

For anyone interested in aviation a landing at Barra "airport"
is high on the bucket list of things to do before you die. The
runway in this case is the cockle strand at Traigh Mhor on
the lovely west coast island. A landing strip is marked out on
the firm sand and once cockle gatherers and sunbathers are
swept off the "runway", and the tide is far enough out, suitable aircraft are cleared to land. Various types, including the
de Havilland *Twin Otters* and *Islanders* operated flights from
Glasgow. One pilot observed that it must be the cleanest runway
in the world since it is washed twice a day. The aircraft, too,
were kept sparkling as splashing though sea water puddles
could cause corrosion and they were given regular cold fresh-
water baths. The potential of Barra's sand as a landing spot
was recognised as early as the thirties. However, Barra is not
unique in having a sand runway as Captain Mac could testify.

In 1967 Angus MacKinnon, the doctor at Northton on the west
tip of Harris rang him at Loganair to say, "Why not call in up
here?" The Harris beach had been used by aircraft before the
Second World War. "I'll give it a go tomorrow," said McIntosh

and instructed the doctor to head to the beach by car and make a few tyre and skid marks to test the sand. Lobster pot floats marked the best track and a windsock was constructed, which lasted despite the vagaries of the Hebridean weather for years. Between 1967 and 1972 the *Piper Aztec, Islanders* and the *Beech 18* regularly used the strip. Dr MacKinnon was rewarded with a free newspaper wrapped in plastic and thrown from the cockpit windows on the days when a landing was not possible, and he got the occasional free flight to Glasgow. Of these days Scott Grier trenchantly remarks that the MacKinnon/Northton runway test procedures never made it into the Civil Aviation Authority handbooks. Scotland is not alone in having sand runways. Pendine in Wales, the site of motor racing world speed record attempts in the thirties, still serves the RAF for rough ground landing training for pilots of the *Hercules C-130*. You could pack a serious number of *Aztecs* into this military freighter.

Another Scottish destination on that proverbial bucket list must be a flight between Westray Airport and Papa Westray Airport in the Orkneys. This is said to be the shortest scheduled flight in the world and the record time for an air trip between the two islands is fifty-three seconds (though the timetable gives you two minutes to allow for headwinds!) and the journey only moves you about the same distance as a jaunt along the runaway at Edinburgh airport. But watch this space. The rush to develop aircraft powered by electricity is on worldwide and several prototypes have taken to the air with success. But, as in the world of the electric car, "range anxiety" is the problem. However, on island hopping in Orkney this will not be a problem and Loganair, with its legendary ability to pioneer, is on the case. But for the moment an *Islander* or similar will have to do. Why go there? Papa Westray's magnificent archaeological sites (around sixty) help fill the seats on the short hop and, of course, the flights are vital in medical emergencies.

Back to the business of building a viable scheduled airline, Captain Mac identified a shortage of landing strips with rather more potential than the odd beach of firm white sand, despite the prevalence of old military airfields left unused after the war and plenty of flat agricultural land that could handle a grass or short tarmac runway. The Royal Engineers did construct some new airfields as part of a plan to use military skills to help and communities such as Plockton, Glenforsa and Broadford on Skye benefitted. And RAF bases at Kinloss, Leuchars, Lossiemouth, Machrihanish, and Arbroath were made available for civilian use on request. In the now almost sixty years of life Loganair survives, despite the eventual financial failure of the construction company that started it all. It has had more changes of ownership, amalgamations, and rebranding than most folk have had hot dinners, as they say in Glasgow. Indeed, I would say firms specialising in aircraft liveries and providing regular new paint jobs owe it a huge debt. But at the time of writing, during the pandemic, with giants like the *A380* and the *B747* heading into retirement, the fact that Loganair is still surviving is the result of more than nimble financial footwork and that astonishing ability to adapt to change – I suspect that teamwork and a love of flying has infused this remarkable little airline with something special. I compare the ethos of that of the treatment of Fresson by the national airline and how Loganair behaved when they took over the Barra route. Part of the agreement was that a legendary figure in the isles, the station superintendent Katie MacPherson was retained as was another fabled islander "Big Archie" McArthur on Tiree.

In *Fate is the Hunter*, some say the greatest book on aviation ever written, Ernest K Gann deliberated thus on the love of flying:

He (a pilot) may pass a motionless airplane without noticing it, but the moment his ears detect a burst of power from a plane, however distant, he will turn his head regardless of everything else around him and watch it. He will also rudely break off in the middle of a conversation to watch a plane landing though there may be a constant flow of them. From observance of such activity he enjoys an abiding satisfaction, as basic and everlasting as that found by a deep-sea sailor on his obligatory pilgrimage to the nearest harbour. Is it not so, then, if there is fascination there must be devotion and joy?

Is it too fanciful to believe that such thoughts have imbued Loganair folk down the years with a special ability to survive in the adventurous, and hard, environment of airline building? I think not.

18

Edinburgh vs Glasgow . . . Rivalry in the Air

Scotland's greatest cities, Edinburgh and Glasgow, have for centuries been locked in rivalry in many fields – sport, particularly football, and all matters cultural. In aviation there is not much doubt that in terms of passengers and flights Edinburgh is the country's number one today. But both cities have a long history of playing a major role in the development of military and commercial flying. These days few of the hundreds of thousands who yearly pass through the modern concourses, bars, restaurants and shops, before padding down a crowded air bridge to the comfort of a modern jet, give little thought to the brave men and women in goggles and leather helmets who took to the clouds in dangerous "stringbags" with few navigational devices and temperamental engines. Now it is all concrete runways, radar and routes thousands of miles long. But it began with under-powered and fragile concoctions of wood and canvas staggering slowly off a grass strip with only a glimpse upwards to blackened rain clouds or at a lonely fluttering windsock as an aid to judging the weather conditions.

First to Glasgow. In the days before Glasgow's airport was given the dignity and importance of being labelled "Glasgow International", Scotland's greatest industrial city had two airports. Abbotsinch, used by the RAF and as a Royal Naval Air Station, named "HMS Sanderling", and Renfrew Airport, a pioneer of civil aviation. Aptly one of the bars in Glasgow Airport today is called the Sanderling. It is a popular place for a pre-flight snifter though you wonder how many of the drinkers recognise the provenance of the name. In 1963 Abbotsinch, a rather boggy piece of land within the fork of the White and Black Cart rivers was transferred to the Ministry of Aviation and opened three years later as Glasgow Airport replacing Renfrew. In due course it used the adjective "international" in its advertising, a move that was highly controversial since millions had been poured into keeping the "fog-free" Prestwick and its immensely long main runway, as a hub for international flights. Safety issues were raised, and much made of Prestwick's geographical advantages – low lying ground for miles around at one end of the main runway and at the other end immediate flight paths over the sea, both good markers for air safety. Though taking off to the west required a swift climb to get over Goatfell and the other peaks of Arran. The new Glasgow Airport had a rail line and a busy highway at one end and high flats close to the other. These days the proximity of the rail line alone might have ruled it out as a suitable sight. The main factor in favour of the new airport was, of course, convenience to Glasgow city centre. The boggy nature of Abbotsinch in its early days led to tales about aircraft disappearing in the mud. I am not sure of that, but I am sure the odd spanner or sparking plug, at least, was dropped by maintenance crews and disappeared under the grass.

HMS Sanderling opened in 1932 and was a grass strip until 1942. Basically, the airfield was used by the RAF and the Navy for coastal patrol work, maintenance, storage and training. Abbotsinch was for many years the home of 602 Glasgow Squadron which flew *Spitfires*. You can appreciate the beautiful lines of this WW2 fighter in Glasgow's Kelvingrove Art Gallery and Museum where a 602 veteran hangs on wires from the roof looking exactly as it did when it went to war. This "Spit" has been restored perfectly after a heavy landing at an English airport in 1949 made it unserviceable. It is thought to be the oldest nonflying *Spitfire* in the world.

As a design the *Spitfire* is, of course, legendary. To watch it fly is to see a remarkable fusion of engineering efficiency and sheer beauty. Again, the adage "if it looks the part, it can usually play it" was never more apt. Those who flew the "Spit", and its similarly beautiful rival, the slightly less lauded *Hurricane*, had a genuine affection for the aircraft.

A true landmark of aviation history, the longevity of the fighter and its development over the years is remarkable. The *Spitfire* first took to the air as long ago as 1934, though it is best remembered for its contribution to the air victory in the Battle of Britain. More than 20,000 were built and one of the final versions – the *Seafire* – was so much more powerful than the early versions that it is claimed that it could have taken off carrying the weights of thirty-two passengers and their luggage! Though there was no space for them! The top speed had also risen from 362 mph to 425 mph. The rate of climb had almost doubled, and the range had gone from 575 miles to 1,475 miles. It is an astonishing rate of development proving that the original design was brilliant.

A remarkable book, *First Light* by Geoffrey Wellum, gives extraordinary insight into the life of a young *Spitfire* pilot in the early forties. It is only a little exaggeration to say that you almost feel you are in the cockpit with him as he tells of aerial dogfights in excellent highly detailed, but not over-wrought, prose. In combat he often flew several sorties a day helping drive the Nazi *Me 109s* fighters and *Heinkel* bombers back across the channel. The *Spitfire* was a beautiful killing machine that the Luftwaffe feared. But it demanded respect from its pilots. The list of Wellum's friends, from training days to actual combat, who died makes sad reading.

The *Spitfire*, of course, was complex and thrilling to fly, but far from as demanding as a modern jet fighter. Early aircraft that flew off the grass field at Abbotsinch were simpler to fly, though there was always danger of mechanical failure. The *Westland Wapitis* biplane and both the *Hawker Hawk* and the *Hawker Hind* were based here. Other early aircraft stationed there included the *Avro Anson*, the *Bristol Beaufort*, and the *Lysander*, much used to drop spies by parachute behind enemy lines. This single-engine high wing monoplane was heavily used by the Special Operations Executive because of its rugged design and short take-off and landing ability. If a landing behind enemy lines was required, rather than dropping a parachutist, it could handle the roughest of ground. The rear cockpit was intended to accommodate one passenger but on occasion three spies were jammed into it. The *Lysander* was a favourite of TV drama makers and shots of it on moonlight excursions to aid the resistance fighters of France were impressive.

The legendary *Tiger Moth* was a frequent sight, unworried about the muddy runways. One "Moth" from Abbotsinch ended its life in what some of imaginative mind call "Scotland's Bermuda Triangle". It is a strange and still largely unexplained fact that between 1938 and 1958 a number of aircraft, said to be around twenty, crashed in the Renfrewshire area that is now Clyde Muirshiel Regional Park, a recreational area that takes in parts of Renfrewshire, Inverclyde, and North Ayrshire with a splendid selection of wildlife, walking paths, visitor centres and sports activities. Why this number of crashes? Abbotsinch and Renfrew flight paths often took planes over this hilly area which was prone to mist. But twenty crashes? Some aviation buffs have suggested that the many mineral deposits in the area might have affected the unsophisticated navigational equipment fitted to early aircraft. Whatever, the *HMS Sanderling Moth* flew into a hill in cloud when on coastal patrol or training flight. The accident happened in May 1940; the same month *Tiger Moths* were withdrawn from coastal patrol work.

I mentioned Muirshiel Park, a place much used by Paisley "buddies" and Glaswegians seeking a Sunday afternoon jaunt in pleasant surroundings. In research for this book, I came across an altogether unusual jaunt to Abbotsinch itself in the sixties which demonstrates a dramatic contrast to the way airports are run these days. Now heavily armed policemen swarm around mingling with tourists and businessmen, there are high hard-to-climb fences topped with barbed wire around the perimeters, plus dog patrols and sophisticated anti-drone devices and security TV cameras. Even the front doors of the terminal have concrete bollards to deter ram raids. But a young Englishman, a student at the nearby Paisley Tech, painted a very different picture of Abbotsinch in the sixties. Brian Farley wrote:

I was on my way home to Cardonald one day on my bike and exploring back roads when I found a farm track which petered out into a path. Eventually I came to a low wire fence with a hut of electronics on the other side. So, I continued the concrete path on the other side, wondering why the concrete was getting wider and wider and then excessively wide. When I saw the control tower I got off fast and cycled through the compound and out the main gate – saluting the Naval guards as I went past. So, to this day, I can truthfully say that I cycled down the main runway at Glasgow Airport! Even the control tower is as I remembered it, but the buildings behind it look totally gone.

Changed days indeed.

The military and naval history of Abbotsinch and its continuing use as an international civilian airport should not overshadow the importance in the development of flying in Scotland of the nearby Renfrew. Today motorists in their millions hurtle down a section of the M8 between Glasgow and Greenock oblivious to the fact that they are on what was the long straight runway of Renfrew airport. The road builders had taken advantage of the smooth and well laid surface of the runway, left behind when the airport closed in 1966, to save a bob or two on the construction budget. Heading towards Glasgow the boy racers on the motorway, if they slowed a little and glanced to the left, could spot a crane or two situated at the old Govan docks, now little used and the home of new housing. In its heyday pilots of BEA *Dakotas, Viscounts, Vanguards* and *Tridents* claimed they flew close enough to see what the crane operators were having on their sandwiches. It may not have been as testing as take-off and landing between the skyscrapers that surrounded the infamous old Hong Kong airport, but it demanded attention.

In the thirties Renfrew was a busy civilian hub. One of the most important airlines using it was the Railway Air Service, a forerunner of BEA (British European Airways) which was formed by the pre-nationalisation "big four" railway companies: London, Midland & Scottish, London & North Eastern, Great Western and Southern Railway. Just as today in the jet age we have feeder airlines and airports, RAS linked up with Imperial Airways international services. The main operating base in the thirties was Croydon, then London's most important civil airfield. The service to Scotland began in 1934 using *Dragon Rapide* biplanes. Unlike the great post-war days of the shuttle, once an hour, it was once a day service heyday RAS was flying *Dakotas*, *Avro Ansons* and somewhat surprisingly the spoils of war in the shape of ex-Luftwaffe *Junkers JU 52 trimotors*. The trusty *DC3* was a favourite on the Glasgow–London service because of its larger passenger capacity.

In the summer of 1946, the government gave BEA the monopoly of flights to United Kingdom and European destinations and in early 1947 the new airline acquired the RAS aircraft and staff. So ended a period in the history of Renfrew which had begun in 1933 with scheduled flights to Campbeltown. Incidentally Angus MacVicar, perhaps Kintyre's most famous author, featured the old airport in a novel called *Return to the Lost Planet* when a character takes the bus from the old terminal in St Enoch Square in Glasgow to Renfrew. Presumably it was a shoogly journey the author had experienced on many a journey from Glasgow to and from Campbeltown.

19

Culture Flown in by the Plane Load

In the battle for aviation ascendancy between Glasgow and the capital, statistics are thrown around with abandon, with the number of movements or the number of destinations pitted against each other. But it is generally a friendly rivalry despite the inevitable commercial competition. There are remarkable similarities in the history of Abbotsinch and Turnhouse. Both had military beginnings. The grass strip off the main Glasgow–Edinburgh Road, on the outskirts of the city was the Royal Flying Corp's most northerly base in World War One. It opened in 1916 and in 1918 with the formation of the Royal Air Force it became a Ministry of Defence property named RAF Turnhouse. Then in 1925 it became home to 603, City of Edinburgh, Squadron.

Early plane spotters in pullovers and tweeds (the anorak has not yet become the favoured dress of notebook-wielding enthusiasts who flocked to airports and railway stations in simpler times) would have seen, like Glasgow, the *Westland Wapitis*, *Hawker Harts* and *Hawker Hinds* chug their spluttering way across the grass and into the air on training sorties. More blood stirring and spectacular were the *Spitfires* of three squadrons based there in the Second World War. Apart from the military connection Turnhouse, like Abbotsinch, was established on a site that because of the closeness to railway and motorways would now be considered as suitable.

Shuttle flights to London, as operated with great success from Glasgow, were also an important part of Turnhouse's history. British European Airways started a service to the "Smoke" from Edinburgh as early as 1947 with the *Vickers Viscount*. Within a few years the turbo-prop *Viscount* and *Vanguard* were the workhorses on the service. As at all the major Scottish airports, Edinburgh went through almost constant upgrading and expansion of the terminals as air travel ceased to be limited to a privileged elite and became a mass market. Aviation in Edinburgh had come a long way from the RFC days at the start, in 1962, of regular international flights from Turnhouse – recent figures showed more than 11m passengers a year used it and flight movements were more than 100,000. Impressive figures helped by the lure of the capital's International Festival and Fringe which yearly draw thousands to a summer orgy of culture.

The first international flights were to Dublin. Interestingly that was the destination, many years later, of a plane which crashed into the sea not long after leaving the airport, killing both pilots. Unlike the major loss of life in the two passenger airliners who crashed on or near Prestwick, recounted earlier, no passengers died. The plane involved, a *Shorts 360*, was for years a successful passenger carrier on short European routes; this plane was a freight carrier, with the passenger seats removed. In February 2001 it had left the capital heading for Dublin in the early evening. It had arrived earlier in snowy and freezing conditions. Not unusual in the city where the locals are wont to complain of the cold winds. Weather was the key to the cause of the tragedy. The *360* had been sitting on the runway for several hours facing into the sleety wind. In this aircraft the engine intakes were higher off the ground than in many other models – around nine feet. That meant the pilots could not see directly into them. With no protective covers fitted, slush had been blown inside the engines unknown to the pilots. The inquiry into the crash concluded that the primary cause was "lack of an established procedure for flight crews to install engine air intake covers in adverse weather conditions."

This seems harsh because it was a tad more complicated than that – as in most accidents there was a combination of factors involved. The intake plugs were not carried as part of the aircraft's on-board equipment. And such plugs were not on hand at the airport at this time. The fact that the engines were too high for manual inspection without ladders was also a factor. A further factor that made the actions of the crew understandable was that "information concerning freezing weather conditions in the aircraft manufacturer's manual had not been included in the airline's *Shorts 360* Operators Manual and were therefore not complied with." But the pilot did all that seemed necessary including extensive engine runs on the ground to clear off any snow or ice that might have accumulated on the intakes. A sad accident.

The take-off was as normal, but at around 2,000 feet changes in the engine air take flow caused by the unseen build-up of slush caused both engines to flare out and the *360* plunged nose down into the Firth of Forth imbedding itself in the sand and killing both pilots. A sad footnote is that the Air Accident Investigation Board found that some years earlier a similar aircraft had suffered from engine failure from the same cause. The report made recommendations to the manufacturers and airlines regarding the use of the *360* in freezing weather. The pilots of that mail flight were not the first to be caught out by snow or slush or icing. And on detailed reading of what happened it is hard to be too critical of the pilots' role in what happened. Snow and slush are ever-present dangers to all pilots.

Another pilot – BEA's James Thain – survived the Munich air disaster which killed twenty-three people, famous international sportsmen and sports reporters returning from a Manchester United European cup-tie in Belgrade. The German authorities blamed Thain saying he did not de-ice the wings, despite eyewitness statements indicating de-icing was not required. He was "let go" as it was put by the airline and spent the next ten years or so trying to clear his name. It was later learned that slush had made it impossible for the *Ambassador* to gain flying speed. Thain was cleared in 1968. He died aged fifty-four.

20

The Skirl of the Pipes, a Touch of Tartan and Financial Woes

A successful airline needs more than planes, pilots, mechanics, stewards, stewardesses, ground staff and passengers! Good marketing is vital. The image of Scotland as a travel destination is appealing for anyone in the flying business trying to get "bums on seats" and cash in the bank. This wee country has an iconic image worldwide. Tenors warbling about "Misty islands of the Highlands", comics with crooked walking sticks, images of a lone piper caught in floodlights on the ramparts of Edinburgh Castle, and the inevitable shortbread tins wrapped in tartan are easy targets for mockery by the sophisticated in the land. They may sneer but the fact is, that in marketing terms the notion that Scotland is, even today, some sort of Brigadoon, works. One American travel writer told his readers that "almost anywhere you look is a subject for a postcard". So, it is no surprise the success of the remodelling of industrial Glasgow as a City of Culture and a major tourist destination testifies to that. Even the Edinburgh Festival is not shy of dropping a touch of tartan into its marketing mix on occasion, so no wonder that airlines have often turned to a drop of heathery hype. The perception of Scotland as a place with a reputation for high educational standards, its own much-admired legal system, and a canny touch in financial matters, has also helped give a feeling of confidence to international travellers and investors thinking of getting into the airline business.

In his excellent history of Loganair, Scott Grier found Scottish names galore, most of which – unlike Loganair, the great survivor – are now relatively forgotten. There was even a Tartan Air Charter operating out of Glasgow, a city hardly noted for "glens and wee but and bens". British Caledonian and Highland Express were two major airlines of the jet age that tried the tartan magic but still drifted out of the headlines. But, along with Loganair, the most important name in the story of the development of air travel within Scotland itself is Highland Airways, based from 1933 in Inverness, not as you might expect Glasgow or Edinburgh. The founder was the legendary Captain Ted Fresson.

It is said the St Petersburg-Tampa Airboat Line (not the catchiest of names!) in Florida was the world's first regularly scheduled passenger airline. Its inaugural flight from the St Pete's yacht basin to Tampa, eighteen miles away, took place in January 1914 – almost thirty years before Highland Airways. The pioneering US line's single plane was a *Benoist* flying boat only twenty-six feet long and powered by a tiny 75hp engine. If the equipment was unimpressive the pilot, Tony Jannus, at least looked the part, in what the local papers called "natty white slacks, dark blazer and bow tie". The flight got up to a mile a minute. Everyone had a window seat. The passenger airliner was in business. But a few months later that year when the "snowbirds" who flee the cold winters of northern states had gone back home from sunny Florida, taking the line's traffic base with them, the airline folded. In its short life it carried 1,200 passengers – at five dollars a flight – without an accident.

The pilot Jannus was a flamboyant character. One history of him declares:

> Tony Jannus desired more than sophistication in his younger days. Once known as a fearless daredevil and an admirer of women, running from angry fathers with pointed shotguns and dating movie stars, Jannus took risks in love and war.

Jannus's charm was as powerful as his bravery and he is described as a "well-bred lovable gentleman". In the year he piloted that first commercial airline flight he once dressed as Santa Claus and parachuted toys to excited kids watching him fly by. He knew a bit about parachutes too, as he had flown the plane from which the world's first parachute jump was made. He also broke altitude records and became the first pilot in the states to carry a passenger. Nicknamed the "bird man" he once won a 10,000 dollar four-cylinder motor air race from St Louis to Omaha with only three cylinders. A breakdown caused him to force land and he repaired the damage with a wooden plug and took off again!

Such an adventurous life was likely to end in disaster for the self-taught aviator. And it did. Jannus' thirst for thrills took him to Sevastopol in 1916. He took two Russians on a flight in a *Curtiss K* flying boat and all three died after a crash caused by engine failure over the Black Sea. The bodies of the passengers were recovered as they were strapped in. Tony Jannus was never found. You suspect such a death was perhaps the sort of end this remarkable man would have known was likely to be his fate someday.

That historic pattern of initial airline success followed by a quicker than expected demise was repeated time after time in the decades that followed as start-ups and the dreams of their pioneer owners and investors crashed down to earth. Over the years the airlines have had almost as many amalgamations, takeovers, and consolidations as passengers. The forerunners of the great international airlines of today were aware of the power of good marketing. In the thirties they spent great sums of money commissioning the top names in commercial art to produce posters advancing the glamour of emerging air travel. Striking examples such as the image of a KLM *Fokker* flying above the ship of the mythical *Flying Dutchman* helped make the airline a world-famous brand. The Italian airlines of the day got together as *Le Linee Aeree d' Italia* using a beautiful image of a flying boat soaring over Mediterranean Italy. England's Imperial Airways were not left behind and pictured wealthy male passengers with raincoats overarm and trilby hats, accompanied by ladies dressed fit for Ascot, emerging after a flight in a *Short Scylla*. This poster highlighted the airline's destinations like . . . Europe, Africa, India, China and Australia.

A world away from this arty glitz Highland Airways was ploughing, was a rather different furrow in bringing air travel to Scotland, particularly the Western Isles, the Orkney and Shetland islands. For the founder of this pioneer airline, Captain Ted Fresson, marketing meant barnstorming round the country in an elderly surplus First World War *Avro 504* biplane. He mixed searching for new territory for his dream airline with demonstrating aerobatics over grass fields and taking locals brave enough on joyrides. He must have piloted thousands on their first flights. Fresson had a vision, but unlike many of the emerging airlines of the era, he did not enjoy joint ventures with other well-healed travel companies. Highland Airways was built up by his solo drive from nothing to an airline that was to have a huge impact on Scotland. Fresson had started the career that made him one of the greatest of British pilots of the early years of aviation as an engineer. It didn't seem a natural choice for the son of a wealthy London stockbroker and a talented pianist whose family ran one of England's most prestigious auction houses. But clearly, he was a success. His firm sent him to their branch in China in 1911 when he was a mere twenty years old. At the start of the First World War in 1914 he returned to Britain to pursue his dream of becoming a pilot and trained with the Royal Flying Corps in Canada.

At the end of the war he went back to China and his job with his old firm. This time he mixed work with his passion for flying. He reassembled or repaired elderly aircraft and used them to ferry local dignitaries round that huge country. He progressed to designing and building his own craft. The buyer was a Chinese warlord and the idea was to put this plane into production. But as the political scene in China became more and more fraught, Fresson returned to Britain in the late twenties and started on a new full-time career as a barnstorming pilot. It was exhilarating and dangerous work that took him all around the country. This was the era when air shows drew large crowds to anywhere with fields flat enough to allow the lumbering craft of the day to bounce across the grass and up and away into the clouds to the wonder of folk who had never seen such a sight. Initially Ted Fresson worked for one of the many companies that toured like travelling circuses – indeed early air shows were called flying circuses – making a living stunt flying and selling joy rides. "Looping the loop" and wing walking, said to have been invented by Charles Lindberg himself, brought gasps of appreciation from the watching crowds. Fresson eventually moved on to form his own company. In the twenties and thirties, between the wars, there was a sort of collective air fever in the travelling public. Most could not afford the ticket prices of the early airlines, but they would turn out in their thousands to watch and dream. The scale of the interest is demonstrated by the success of the pioneer long distance aviator, Alan Cobham. When not breaking international distance records he toured the length and breadth of Britain with his National Aviation Day displays. This was no lone biplane putting on a show. Cobham had as many as fourteen different aircraft demonstrating their abilities. This was a big money enterprise.

A spin-off was that pilots like Fresson gained a deep knowledge of the geography of these isles and the potential for a reliable airline to bring new life to remote communities. It is said of his knowledge of Scotland that he was never more than a few miles away from a field he had the skill to land on. The government tapped into this knowledge during the Second World War and used Fresson as an advisor on airfield locations and the construction of runways and other airport buildings. One of the sites he suggested was for an airport at Inverness which is still in successful use today. He also pioneered the use of tarmac for runways as even in the early days of aviation in Scotland, planes were rapidly becoming heavier and heavier. Landing strips he constructed at Stornoway (care was taken to minimise the effect on the golfers of Lewis) and at Hatston in Orkney are regarded by many aviation historians as the first true runways in Britain.

Many years earlier, in 1933, this remarkable man had started scheduled services in Scotland, a country that he had developed a great liking for as a place that suited his style. The initial flights of Highland Airways were in May between Inverness, Wick and Kirkwall. In 1934 the fledgling airline made history by being awarded the first airmail contract by the Post Office which required him to fly mail at ordinary rates to Orkney and back. In the autumn of the previous year, he made another little bit of history operating the first commercial charter out of Aberdeen, ferrying three intrepid salesmen to Shetland. It is hoped these adventurous commercial travellers got orders good enough to reward their initiative.

The Fresson story is intriguing in that although as earlier he did not have the backing of rail or road companies, his vision was clear enough to wring out backing from locals in the areas he was servicing – he got the support of *The Scotsman* newspaper, an Inverness firm of motor engineers, other local traders and even a well-known medical man Dr Alexander of Gray's Hospital in Elgin. Fresson's enthusiasm for flying could be infectious. But not everyone in the Highlands shared his dream; ferry operators and others saw the growth of air travel in Scotland as a threat to revenue streams.

He faced competition himself from a rival, Aberdeen Airways, which started up a year or so after Fresson and rivalled him particularly on the Shetland route. The line changed its name early on to Allied Airways and was best known using this name. This airline was run by an entrepreneur called Eric Leslie Gandar Dower who was largely responsible for the creation of Aberdeen airport. And in true capitalistic style the competition helped the development of air travel in the far north of Scotland. Gandar Dower's Allied was a real competitor to Fresson and developed services between Aberdeen and Shetland. His celebrated pilot was Eric Starling who became a leading figure in BEA's Scottish history. It is hard not to wonder at the bravery and ingenuity of the pilots of these pioneer airlines. Landings and take-offs were into and from "airports" which in truth were mostly level farm fields cleared of dykes and loose boulders, with livestock often shuffled into nearby areas as the aircraft approached. As was the case in all parts of Britain aerial navigation was pretty hit and miss, especially in bad weather and low visibility. Tales of pilots navigating by looking down and following railway lines are not far-fetched. Indeed, it is said that a lost pilot or two solved the problem by swooping down to read the names on country station notice boards. Incidentally the pilots called the rail tracks "the iron compass". Some even dropped down to see if the washing lines were out and it really was Monday. Such navigation was ok in the populous and wealthy southeast of Britain, but in the Highlands and Islands, railway stations and washing lines are hard to find. Airlines such as those run by Dower and Fresson found the navigation problems eased a bit by the introduction of ratio let down in 1934.

In Fresson's autobiography *Air Road to the Isles* he describes the process making it sound much less daunting than it was in real life: "The radio station simply brought the aircraft over-head by a series of wire telegraphy bearings (using Morse code) or radio telephony if no radio officer was aboard. After that, the pilot had to find his own way down and on to the airfield". That's all then! Fresson goes on to remark that with practise "we got extremely accurate with the let down and could get into our airfield with the cloud a few feet off the deck and with visibility a few hundred yards or so." No mention that this often took place in horizontal rain or sleet with the bitter wind howling in from the west fresh off the Atlantic. The regularity and timekeeping records of these early airlines is astonishing considering the relatively primitive state of aircraft design, the lack of modern navigational aids and the fact that the pilots did not benefit from the sophisticated satellite-aided weather fore-casting of today. Fresson was particularly successful in winning mail contracts and of course spotting good land for airfields. There were no scheduled flights within the Orkneys from the end of the Second World War till 1967 when Loganair started the inter-islands air service with its new *Britten Norman Islander* using several of the North Isles airstrips which were used by Fresson almost thirty years earlier.

There is a shameful coda to the Fresson story. His airline was eventually part of the post-war British Airways. Previously Northern and Scottish Airways based at Renfrew had merged with Highland to form United Airways in the thirties. Northern and Scottish flew to Skye and the Uists and other spots in the Western Isles; Fresson territory. It was founded by a former bus operator from Newcastle. In the early thirties some road transport organisations were dipping a toe in the growing aviation scene. Even the mighty SMT (Scottish Motor Traction) briefly had an aviation department though it did not survive long. Travellers using Northern and Scottish were picked up at Glasgow's famed Central Hotel, next to Central Station, and taken by road to Renfrew to catch their flights.

After the creation of British European Airways at the end of the Second World War Ted Fresson was astonishingly "let go" without financial compensation in 1948. He was not alone – several other pioneer aviators who created the airlines that were nationalised were treated in similar shabby fashion. Ted Fresson had created a network of air travel to the benefit of the folk in some of the most far-flung parts of Britain. It was a network still basically in use today. No matter his feelings on how he was treated, Fresson continued his love affair with flying by taking charter flights around and about the Highlands and Islands using his own light aircraft. He died in Inverness in 1963. His contribution to the development of flying cannot be underestimated and certainly not forgotten.

The pioneer airline builders of Scotland were only the first to try to use the romantic image of the Highlands and the sometimes Gaelic speaking, sometimes tartan clad, inhabitants of the often rainswept hills and glens to help fill passenger planes with tourists. Even in the jet age, marketeers saw the somewhat exaggerated folksy picture of Scotland peddled in the brochures as a useful tool to fill seats. Perhaps, too, the more realistic image conjured up by the phrase "Clyde built" and a general perception of competent heavy industry helped. Whatever, pipers in full tartan dress were in demand for photo opportunities as new routes opened and new airlines were born and died.

Highland Express was a name that sounded good and conjured up all the right thoughts in a would-be passenger's mind. As did Caledonian Airways (more on it later). But there was a major flaw in the dream behind Highland Express. The giant tail fin of a *Boeing 747*, painted with a proud Saltire, stood out well on the crowded airport forecourts on both sides of the Atlantic. But the problem was that the Highland Express "fleet" consisted of only one plane! Of course, the plan was to add more aircraft as the airline grew. But, in hindsight, it seems obvious, even to those not close to the problems of scheduling, timetabling and maintaining a transatlantic service, that there was, as they say, trouble ahead . . .

The airline had been formed in 1984 and experienced ground and flight staff recruited, but the first flights did not take place until May 1987. The folly of relying on a single aircraft was demonstrated from day one. The plan was to fly from Prestwick to New York (Newark), London (Stanstead and Gatwick), Brussels and Toronto. The official launch was to be on the day of the Prestwick International air show, good PR. In fact, the first flight took place a few days before the weekend air show (which for years was a well-loved event for aviation buffs and their families). The plane used was a hired ex-*Cargolux 747-200* as a leased

Jumbo had not yet been delivered. The substitute plane was a bit of a compromise. The tartan uniforms of the cabin crew may have looked dandy, but the plane itself, adapted for passenger use, was somewhat tired. The passengers on the official inaugural flight a day or two later enjoyed to the full the complementary, and for such an occasion, a cynic might observe, obligatory, free bar service. But those with return tickets might not have been in such a merry mood as they ploughed their way across the Atlantic if they knew what lay ahead. Highland Express was forced to pay for seats home for them on an American airline, Northwest.

It was just the first of many frustrations faced by travellers with the new airline. A hoped licence for flights to Canada, a prime target for taking a slice of the Scottish diaspora market, heavily mined by Air Canada and others, did not materialise, creating a big hole in the business plan. Inevitable mechanical problems with a "fleet" comprising of a single aircraft also caused financial problems. Chartering a replacement *Jumbo* does not come cheap. Highland Express went down the tubes before the end of the year.

The now almost forgotten airline has one claim to fame – it was one of the first low fare carriers. Though far from as successful as others like Ryanair and easyJet who made cheapo flights pay using sheer volume and introducing extras such as paying for luggage and drinks and snacks. Back in the autumn of 1987 you could get to London Stanstead from Prestwick for the sum of a mere £19 (a few quid more for first class). A brave Scottish airline that did not take off. The "fleet" of one *Jumbo* was sold to Virgin and then scrapped.

In its brief life this overambitious venture certainly played the tartan card in its public relations, but its campaign was much less memorable, or successful, than that of another airline of the sixties, seventies, and eighties – British Caledonian. You don't need to be an aviation anorak to remember its powerful TV advertising. The B-Cal ads, I suspect, appear a tad sexist in retrospect. But more than forty years ago they were effective and generally regarded as a bit of fun. Some say they were inspired by the music of the Beach Boys. There was a zippy jingle that had some leering male customers, in airport departing areas, singing "I wish they all could be Caledonian Girls" – a clear, if jokey, reference to the attractiveness and professionalism of the B-Cal "girls" over those working for other airlines. The Caledonian Girls in the ads, of course, were far from the matronly types you might encounter on the US airlines, of the era who didn't dump female cabin staff when they were out of their twenties. The TV Caledonian Girls wouldn't have been out of place in the popular swimming pool beauty queen contests so popular at the time. And did they wear tartan? You bet! These days you can design and register your own new tartan as Rangers football club and others have done. But B-Cal had their own design run up when there was a tartan free for all. And they also used other tartans in variations on the cabin staff uniforms. These TV ads would now no doubt be frowned on by the politically correct regiments that comb the airways these days looking for offence, but it was all done with a degree of humour aided by that catchy jingle that made it good advertising.

British Caledonian had its roots in a charter operation out of Prestwick in the early sixties. But it really took off after a merger with British United Airways. The tall tail fin of the modern jet is a potent place to advertise your airline. Millions of pounds or dollars and millions of working hours in advertising agencies are spent on making decisions on how best to use this metal "canvas". Highland Express chose a saltire theme to add to their tartan style while British Caledonian used a Lion Rampant.

Sometimes the simple is best and a good example is Qantas. It didn't take a genius to realise that when an Australian airline with the lengthy moniker of Queensland and Northern Territory Aerial Services Limited decided to go into the international business the ideal way to deliver the message, without the need for words, was a giant kangaroo painted on to the tail fin. Likewise, for Caledonian, that proud golden lion was the ideal image to use in the airline's livery. Qantas is the third oldest major airline in the world (After KLM and Avianca), founded in the twenties, and for almost 100 years the "flying kangaroo" as it became known has worked hard for it, building a great reputation.

B-Cal never had the international success or reach of the Australian giant, but for a time in the eighties it came close to rivalling it in the size of its fleet and number of employees. In its heyday it operated from Scotland, London, Amsterdam and Newcastle as well as having networks in South America and Africa. Like Qantas, B-Cal had an enviable safety record and never lost a paying passenger. Though it nearly did in one remarkable air incident that has seldom been equalled by a passenger jet. Of enormous significance, the plane involved in what could have been a large loss of life was a *VC10*. Its design differed from the early long-haul jets of the American manufacturers. Instead of all the engines being hung under the wing on pods, the *Vickers* airliner was similar to the short-haul jets of the time – like the *BAC 1–11* – which often put the engines at the tail. This layout "cleaned" up the wing which helped ease the climb to cruising height. Two further advantages were that the engines were higher above the runway and their noise was less annoying to the passengers. The higher position of the engines was particularly helpful to B-Cal since their networks often used less well-developed runways in

Africa and South America. The four engine *VC10's* ability to land and take off more slowly than the early *Boeing 707s* was important in such circumstances.

The incident, which became almost legendary in aviation circles, happened in the autumn of 1971. The plane involved was en route from Santiago to London via Buenos Aires. On the first leg of the journey, at almost 30,000 feet, it was just clearing the top of the snow-covered Andes when it hit CAT (clear air turbulence, a phenomenon just becoming recognised at the time) and the jet was thrown on its side at an angle of more than ninety degrees. The flight controls were knocked out and the *VC10* plunged down toward the jagged peaks. There was little time or airspace for the pilots to regain control. And the big jet, approaching the speed of sound, was in a steep dive. Uncontrolled contact with the terrain seemed unavoidable. Somehow the pilots managed to reactivate the flight controls, levelling the jet out, and the flight continued to Buenos Aires where it landed safely. The only causality was a stewardess working in the galley who had received minor injuries. It could have been so much worse – it was the closest of close calls and all on board must have been terrified.

It is a tribute to the strength of the *Vickers* aircraft that after inspection at Buenos Aires it could continue to London. At Gatwick damage to a spar in the tail area was found and lengthy repairs needed. The engineers concluded that in such dramatic circumstances underwing mounted engines would have snapped off causing a massive crash. The *VC10* continued for many years providing excellent service to any airline that had invested in it. My own memory of flying in it was far from as fraught as that downward plunge over the Andes. Like many others I found the air conditioning less than perfect. I remember flying many sweaty summer hours over the Atlantic and watching the drops of condensation sliding down the inside of the cabin. Uncomfortable but not dangerous.

Running a successful airline is a team business. But it is remarkable when you delve back into the history of airline building how often the driving force is one single-minded man who had the brains and bravery to be a great pilot himself and, as his career progressed, the ability to morph into a major player in high finance and big business. Ted Fresson was one such, another was Sir Adam Thomson who built British Caledonian. Thomson, who died in 2000, was even as chairman of the airline, a far from flamboyant figure. But he loved planes and flying, and as a young teenager was inspired by the Battle of Britain.

The son of a railway man, engineering seemed a good choice of career and he enrolled in the renowned Glasgow "Tech", a forerunner of Strathclyde University. Thomson saw this as way into the RAF, and a life in aviation. When he found that the Fleet Air Arm and the Navy would take him earlier than the Air Force he changed plans. But when he was just about to take to the air, a qualified pilot, the war was over. He took this as an opportunity, and he started a small "airline" planning to fly tourists to remote areas. That did not turn out to be even a tiny goldmine and he was forced to turn to regular airline work. It is somewhat ironic that the line that gave him work was British European Airlines which in later years with British Caledonian making its place in British flying turned out to be the opposition. BEA, too, did not meet his expectations and he turned to Africa for regular work, flying for several airlines.

On the ground in remote and often basic airports there was plenty of time to ponder the future. These days it is obvious that a mix of long and short haul, with suitable planes for each, and scheduled and charter services, particularly if you could lower the cost of flying, was the way to go. With a few friends Thomson scrambled together seed money of little more than £50,000 and so began Caledonian Airways. Try that now and you are talking millions even before a first hop. Thomson was the sole pilot and his steed a plane leased from Sabena of Belgium. Charters carrying such as Scots and American family clubs and immigrants from the West Indies helped put the wee Scottish operation on a strong financial base after its low-key start and in the 1960s it grew swiftly.

In the later years of the last century amalgamations dominated the scene, apart from the growth of BEA and British Overseas Airway Corporation, as smaller lines fought to compete with the national giants. Adam Thomson got the break he needed in 1970. A lively smallish but well-liked line, British United Airways was a target for BOAC but Thomson the businessman, now chairman, talked the government into allowing him to buy United. The merger required money and Caledonian became a public company and raised funds for what was to be British Caledonian. It was an opening gambit in a political war over the future of aviation in these islands. The Labour Party was uneasy and angry about this sale to the private sector and went as far as to threaten to take the airline back into public owner-ship when it was returned to power. In the changing world of politics, with the leadership of both main parties fighting their corner fiercely, in the end the opposite happened, and British Airways was privatised. Interestingly, after BA took over British Caledonian in 1987, the government imposed conditions that prevented the operation of Edinburgh and Glasgow routes to Gatwick. Sensing an opportunity, Loganair acquired two *BAe 146* jets that would have suited the routes but the government awarded them to Air UK, causing some financial problems for the Scottish airline.

It was, however, not to end well for the new British Caledonian. After some years of great success, with setbacks in the fraught financial climate of the late eighties, it set about looking for a merger to secure its future. In 1987 British Airways took control. Another dream was over.

21

The Greatest Pilot of Them All?

The folk of the Borders are independent-minded people, proud of the beauty of their countryside and their heritage, particularly that of the Reivers. Every year in towns like Selkirk, Hawick and others there is to be seen the unforgettable sight of the Common Riding where the descendants of those lawless rustlers of the Middle Ages ride out from cobbled streets onto rolling farmland to mark the old borders on horseback, recreating the Riding of the Marches. A wonderful spectacle for tourists, but much more than that, it is a community gathering together to celebrate their identity. The Reivers were hard people who acted hard in hard times and kept a "calm sooch" in an emergency. It is said that in a battle they were ruthless enough to change sides when the winner became obvious.

So, it is maybe no surprise that Neil Armstrong seemed to have the same ability to keep unruffled in the face of imminent disaster. For the first man on the moon claimed Scottish descendants, and when he visited Langholm in 1972, the traditional home of Clan Armstrong, he accepted the honour of being the town's first and only Freeman and remarked that he thought of it as his hometown. And the association with the Borders has done the area nothing but good. The manager of the Clan Armstrong Centre near Langholm thinks that the links to the first man on the moon have been of immense value. He was quoted as telling a national newspaper that: "The number of people, Americans included, who want to experience a visit and witness the astonishing splendour that beholds the birthplace of Neil Armstrong's family is staggering, and helpful to the local economy." And plans are underfoot for festivities to mark the fiftieth anniversary, in 2022, of the astronaut's visit. With the current increasing scientific interest in searching for life elsewhere in the universe, maybe what Armstrong had to say on the subject will chime with the times. Though, if that is the case, I guess he might not be displeased by any revelations.

In correspondence, quoted in a new book by a biographer, the spaceman told a Scot who wrote to him on the subject of alien life that: "On all the manned and unmanned flights to the moon, no evidence has been found which supports the existence of, or visits by any living creatures. No water, no hydrogen or carbon has been found, except at molecular level. There is increasing interest in returning to the moon in the future, so perhaps I will be proven wrong!" The recent science seems to suggest that the clues to alien life would not be found on our near neighbour the moon, but on the distant planets. But it would be interesting, and helpful to Scottish tourism if any new discoveries in the entertainingly controversies anent UFOs emerged.

So, Scotland has links with the most famous flight of all time. And a candidate for the title of the greatest pilot ever is a Scot – Captain Eric "Winkle" Brown who died in 2016 and is said to have flown more types of aircraft than any other flier, surviving eleven crashes. And he had a lot in common with Armstrong.

Both were aircraft carrier men and Navy test pilots. After they first met, they became friends. Though the meeting was embarrassing for Brown. He told a Radio Four documentary that: "In fact when I met Neil, to my horror I didn't really recognise him. He said, 'Well I am a naval aviator like you, and I've heard of your deck landing exploits.' I am talking to the guy who is the top dog of the lot and he knows me, and I don't recognise him. How embarrassing. Here was a man who touched the hand of God. And yet modest beyond words, so modest in fact that he didn't want to talk about it."

Modesty was also a characteristic of Eric Brown. The nickname "Winkle", a shortened version of periwinkle, came from the fact that he was only five foot seven tall. This lack of height was important since he could curl his short legs up under him, something he believed saved his legs in crashes. In that BBC interview, he said that test flying required a certain type of personality. It seemed he had a type shared with Armstrong who even before he became an astronaut had demonstrated a cool head in several emergencies. Brown told his interviewer that, 'I have a nature that doesn't panic. My brain goes very sort of cold and is very good at considering things.' Which it is just as well considering he flew 487 types of different aircraft in his career. In addition, he was the Navy's most decorated test pilot. One of the exploits referred to by Neil Armstrong was in 1945 when he became the first person to land a jet on a carrier. "Winkle" was modest as he looked back on a flying career which took off when his pilot dad took him on lap on a biplane and young Eric was hooked. That innate modesty showed through when in his nineties he remarked he had finally "buckled down to domestic life".

The concept of looking for "the greatest pilot" is as flawed as comparing great golfers of different eras but can be fun. And another candidate for the top spot is a Glaswegian called Jim Mollison, one half of a couple known as *The Flying Sweethearts* in the popular press of the thirties. The other half was the first Mrs Mollison the famed aviator Amy Johnson. Jim Mouison was born in 1905 in Glasgow, the only son of a well-heeled engineer. As a youngster he was educated at both Glasgow and Edinburgh Academies. His father was an apparently unattractive character over fond of the bottle – a hint of what was to happen at the end of Jim's own life – and he disappeared to Australia leaving Jim to be brought up in Scotland by his mother who came from a wealthy shipping family. Jim grew up at a time when Britain's flying pioneers were competing to break records as the aircraft they flew grew in sophistication. Mollison developed a fascination with flying and determined to walk in the footsteps of the daring men and women who were filling the papers with tales of exploits crossing oceans and conquering the highest mountains. His own record breaking started early. When he joined the Royal Air Force on a short service commission he was the youngest officer in the service at eighteen. Just four years later he became an instructor at the Central Flying School and again he was the youngest man to fill that role. Restless, as ever, he joined the RAF reserve and began to concentrate on civil aviation. From 1928 he served as an instructor with two of Australia's early airlines, Eyre Peninsula Airways and Australian National Airways. He thrived in the role and seemed extremely capable at passing his skills on to others. It was a busy life but the young Scot, perhaps with inherited genes beginning to kick in, found time to earn the soubriquet "playboy", not a label much in use in Aussie flying circles of the time. It was from Australia that he began a remarkable career as a record breaker.

As early as 1931 he flew back to the UK in the record time of eight days, nineteen hours (whaurs your *Concorde* now?).

During his time with Australian National he had met Amy
Johnson who was internationally famed at the time for her own
record-breaking exploits. It was love at first sight apparently,
since he proposed only eight hours after meeting her while they
were still in the air. Decisiveness was clearly one of his virtues.
Back on home soil the record breaking continued apace, and
notable flights were the first solo east to west Atlantic crossing
from Portmarnock to New Brunswick. Also memorable was a
record-breaking jaunt to Brazil via Africa in three days and thirteen hours. Both Amy and Jim seemed to enjoy the dangerous,
glamourous, and headline-grabbing early days. They both
looked the part with a touch of Hollywood style, but there was
true substance to their fame. Amy managed to beat Jim's record
to South Africa, stirring the pot of their rivalry. But some joint
flights were made together and in 1933 they lifted off from
Pendine Sands in Wales and headed non-stop for New York.
They ran out of fuel, over Connecticut, not far short of their
destination. Both were injured in a crash landing, not seriously,
but they had the indignity of their craft being torn apart by
souvenir hunters trying to make a quick buck.

The double act of Jim Mollison and Amy Johnson was not
to end well. In the years running up to the Second World War
both continued to set records but the marriage came under
strain both from their rivalry in the air and the fact that Jim
Mollison was taking at times a bigger interest in where his next
drink was coming from, rather than what record to break next.
But both Jim and Amy were particularly suited for a role in the
Air Transport Auxiliary, an organisation charged with ferrying
needed aircraft to various war zones. The flying sweethearts
were by now not so sweet on each other, but both were daring
pilots with vast experience of different types of aircraft, perfect
for a role in the ATA.

Amy generated plenty of "ink" as journalists like to put it, but a less publicised young Scot called Winifred Drinkwater was also record breaking in the thirties. As a teenager, she became the first woman to gain a commercial pilot's licence in 1932. She flew passengers in the early Glasgow-London flights and made an aerial search of Loch Ness in search of the monster. Without success. She was known in aviation circles as the "Scottish Amy Johnson".

Sadly, Amy was killed in 1941. She had set off from Prestwick, a major hub for moving aircraft around Britain, and from the US, in wartime, to fly to the southeast of England. It was January and the weather was far from suitable. Her *Airspeed Oxford* strayed from the planned flight path and it was thought that she ran out of fuel over the Thames estuary. She was forced to parachute out and ships in the busy shipping area saw her alive in the water calling for help in heavy seas with a strong tide flowing and snow falling. The captain of a navy ship, Lieutenant Commander Walter Fletcher, got his vessel close to her in the swells and ropes were thrown in her direction, but she was unable to reach them, and Fletcher dived into the icy water. But he could not save her, and she was swept to her death. The brave sailor was hauled out of the water but died later from exposure. Amy's body was never recovered. A very sad ending indeed. But the story was not quite over. More than fifty years later, in 1999, evidence emerged that Amy was the victim of friendly fire. An RAF man reported that her plane was spotted off course and challenged, but when contacted by radio there was a mix up with the identification code and she was shot down as an enemy aircraft. The RAF man said that they were told not to discuss the incident. And that seems possible since shooting down our own flying sweetheart would not have been welcome news in wartime. Tragedy indeed.

Meanwhile Jim was doing sterling work as a ferry pilot. He, too, was shot down but by the Nazis, rather than his own side. Flying an *Anson* with twelve passengers and crew, he was intercepted by Luftwaffe fighters but managed to land without anyone being hurt. Another exciting flight was to Fort Lamy in Chad, delivering a plane fitted out as personal transport for General de Gaulle. He was awarded an MBE for his services as a ferry pilot and remarried in 1949. But sadly, he lost his battle with the bottle and died a decade later.

22

Heading West and North –
Scotland and the Final Frontier

In the tragic and dramatic months of Covid, readers of Scotland's papers, heavy with page after page endlessly stuffed with the horrors of the pandemic, would be forgiven if they missed the growing coverage of Scotland's somewhat surprising progress as a major player in the space age. The country where Percy Pilcher made his first experiments in flight is quietly building a state-of-the-art industry in satellites and vertical launching technology. Aviation historian Dugald Cameron, with colleagues, wrote a splendid book some years ago with the inspired title of *From Pilcher to the Planets*. Well, we are not quite there yet, though robots are currently trundling around in 'the dusty floor of the red planet.' Maybe, just maybe, a man-made machine will find traces of life. Sarah Stewart Johnson, an assistant professor of planetary science at Georgetown University in the United States, has pointed out the importance of this search on Mars. It is not just that finding so much as a dormant speck of protein in this planetary tomb would be a peerless scientific wonder. It is that if life can emerge and survive on the red planet – "the smallest breath in the deepest night, then it can do so in a trillion other places." It would be proof that we are not alone. But who would have thought that when humans set foot on the planets, some of the knowledge that put us there may have come from the peat-covered acres of the Moine peninsula in remote northern Scotland? Percy Pilcher would have approved.

What is going on in Sutherland and plans for space bases at Machrihanish, Prestwick and other Scottish sites is talked about as something completely new and with the potential to make history. The fact is that almost ninety years ago the Western Isles were the site of rocket experiments designed "to bring the world together". This seems to have slipped off the radar of 2022's scribes in awe of recent developments. That "bringing together" talked of in 1934 was the trial of "The Western Isles Rocket Post". The man behind the idea was a German inventor called Gerhard Zucker. Before coming to Scotland, he was experimenting with an idea to send a rocket with a cargo of mail across the English Channel in just one minute. But coming to the Western Isles his test set him a rather less ambitious target. The plan was to send rocket mail (and packages) from Harris to the tiny island of Scarp, a mere half mile away.

Zucker, it is said, got the idea of rocket travel after reading about a Scarp woman who was airlifted to hospital after complications during the birth of her twin daughters. The first was born on Scarp and the mum flown to Stornoway where the second was delivered. The newspapers of the day knew a good story when they saw one and the girls became Miss Harris and Miss Lewis. The tale set the inventor thinking that maybe a rocket was the answer to the problem of getting medical supplies to far-flung locations in a hurry. He told a *Scotsman* reporter that rocket transport would be a boon to the islands.

The test took place on the beach on Harris, with Scarp looking close enough to be hit by a stone lobbed by a local strong man. It should have been easy meat for a rocket. A sizeable crowd gathered on the beach in expectation of witnessing a break-through in airmail.

The rocket itself was claimed large enough to contain 4,000 letters and some packages, though it must be said looking at old photographs of it, that seemed a tad optimistic. The letters were addressed to such luminaries as King George V and Prime Minister Ramsay MacDonald, and franked Western Isles Rocket Post though the chance of such luminaries being on Scarp to open them was, to put it mildly, remote. What followed was an anti-climax. The device that was to revolutionise airmail exploded, scattering singed letters onto the surf-washed beach. A later second attempt was a repeat of the disaster. The *Press and Journal* reported that: "There was a flash of fire, a cloud of smoke and when the air cleared, the letters were strewn about the wreckage of the firing apparatus." The remnants of some of the letters can still be seen in a museum on Harris.

The inventor returned to his lair in Germany to continue his career as a rocketeer. But the explosions on Harris were not the only Zucker failures, however they were still less deadly than some of his later experiments which caused three fatalities.

In the Second World War Zucker had a hand in the develop-ment of Hitler's *Vengeance* rocket bombs that took a high toll of life in London and southern England. Ironically the focus on sending lifesaving medical supplies to remote islands had changed to one of throwing deadly *V1* rocket bombs at a civilian population. But, of course, the achievement of putting a man on the moon was built on the work of Zucker and others obsessed with rockets. The most important of them was the SS member Werner Von Braun who created the *V* weapons at Peenemunde and who was secretly taken to the United States to work on what was now cynically called "the way to the stars" rather than the way to win a war. I was surprised to read recently in a *National Geographic* publication that: "Von Braun's wartime role as designer of the *V-2* vengeance rocket for Hitler was overshadowed by his contribution to the American space programme for which he received the National Medal of science". Not a verdict that a Londoner would appreciate.

The aforementioned Gerhard Zucker, by background a professional scientist, was not the only experimenter in the off-the-page idea of rocket mail. At home in Scotland, in the douce town of Paisley (world renowned for the large-scale production of linen and thread) in the thirties a remarkable enthusiast called John Stewart was at work on the same dream. He was by far from alone in his fascination with rockets, indeed to this day around the world there are folk who experiment in the backyard construction of projectiles which may look like the magnificent rockets that blast off from Florida or the Russian steppes but are tiny. They fly them in the way that model aircraft makers fly their powered replicas.

John Stewart caught the rocket bug as a schoolboy and voracious science fiction reader. While most boys of his age were immersed in comics such as the *Beano* or *Dandy*, he was spending pocket money on magazines such as *Air Wonder Stories*. He was an early member of the British Interplanetary Society founded in 1933 – the legendary Arthur C. Clarke, science fiction writer and futurologist, signed his membership receipt. When a pupil at the town's prestigious John Neilson Institution, Stewart formed a science fiction club with a handful of friends with similar literary tastes. He soon decided to take the next step of building his own rocket, a move influenced by an early article in the Interplanetary Society's journal. So, the Paisley Rocketeers were born.

Arthur C. Clarke was a member. One small step etc! And a very small step it was . . . the purchase of a few penny fireworks rockets from a local "Jennie A' Things" shop in Paisley's Caledonia Street. The rocketeers were a small enthusiastic group of Paisley "buddies" who spent the years up to the Second World War doing all sorts of experimenting with their models. John Stewart's *Research Rocket 1* consisted of several fireworks in a pointed tube with cardboard fins. Released in a back garden it got lift-off and sent local kids scattering after a swift descent. Mr Stewart (a draughtsman) was a careful hoarder of detailed drawings of his projectiles and reports on the successes or failures of his experiments, all rockets labelled *RR* up to almost *RR100*. Helped by his brother Peter, and many friends and fellow enthusiasts, he was constantly improving and developing the idea of the commercial use of rockets. Like Zucker, it was something of an obsession. Also like the German they had a go, without real success, of firing mail rockets across narrow highland inlets.

That purchase from Annie Howat's shop could, however, have helped lead the world on the way to the moon. Far-fetched as it sounds, the Paisley Rocketeers were the first to use what is now accepted rocket practice . . . the three-stage rocket. Some space historians consider it significant. The Scottish projectiles may have only reached a few hundred feet or so fired from parks and fields around Paisley, but they demonstrated a concept and the realisation that most of the power used in the initial stage of a launch was dead weight that should be discarded shortly after lift-off, and subsequent stages ignited one after another. *Stewart's RR 47* was launched from St James Park in Paisley and has been claimed to be the world's first three-stage rocket.

The Paisley rocketeers, founded in 1936, were disbanded at the start of World War Two but reformed in 1966. And like their innovative use of the three-stage principle they also used parachutes in their experiments with rocket mail. Again a method that NASA and the Russians used to recover returning astronauts. The rocketeers put their ideas to good use sending "rocket mail" on short blasts upwards and recovered the letters and franked them to be sold to stamp collectors and locals to make money for charity. It is truly remarkable that the Paisley enthusiasts also managed to use cameras fitted to the later more sophisticated models to bring back aerial views. It may have been amateur science, but it was obviously really good fun as the smiling faces in the photographs of the launches from Renfrewshire's parks and fields show. The story of this bunch of amateurs left me with the thought . . . what could have happened if, rather than gather together a group of Nazi war criminals to help them in the Space Race, America had shipped the Paisley Rocketeers to Houston and Florida en mass and set them to work backed by the billions of US tax dollars.

Over the last few years Scotland's newspapers have gradually latched on to the fact that this "great little country" which played such an important role in the development of aviation has more than just a toehold in the commercialising of the space race. Along with Elon Musk and his adventures with Space X, Jeff Bezos and the ubiquitous Richard Branson and his Virgin Galactic brand, Scotland has less spectacularly been at the forefront of taking the exploitation of the final frontier out of the hands of a NASA monopoly. Although currently operating in America, Branson made a bold attempt as far back as 2006 to build a spaceport in Scotland at RAF Lossiemouth. He was even talking of launching from Scotland in 2010, but the bearded wonder is always on the optimistic side. It didn't happen, despite the support of local MPs who saw the benefits to be had by adopting such an out-of-the-box idea. There were also talks with the Scottish and UK governments on the potential of commercial space flights. Lossiemouth was among eight short-listed sites in Britain. "Lossie", and nearby RAF Kinloss, were eventually ruled out largely due to opposition from the Military of Defence. A shame . . . Spaceport Lossiemouth has an appealing ring to it. But thanks to that controversial character Branson, Scotland has already had a man in space.

Dave Mackay born in Helmsdale, in Sutherland, a county now the focus of much of Scotland's space hopes, piloted an early test flight of Branson's Virgin Galactic's commercial *SpaceShipTwo* which took him out of the earth's atmosphere. This made him the 569th person to enter space. Back on solid ground Dave said: "I just enjoyed a pretty amazing flight which was beyond anything any of us has ever experienced. It was thrilling yet smooth and nicely controlled throughout with a view at the top of the earth – which exceeded all of our expectations."

In England as far back as the sixties the *Black Arrow* rocket was tested on the Isle of Wight, though it was launched from Woomera in the far north of South Australia around 300 miles from Adelaide. Though the test range had its eye on the skies and space it is close to wealth to be garnered underground – the opal fields of Coober Pedy in places lie under the range. The project was abandoned in 1971 when the UK government decided it was cheaper to hitch a ride on a NASA vehicle rather than do space on our own. Like most rocket testing, some untoward happenings occurred "down under" when one *Black Arrow* launch ended with a crash landing near the pleasant peaceful city of Adelaide rather than reaching near space. The wreckage lay rusting and vandalised for almost fifty years until 2019 when it was shipped to Penicuik in Midlothian and put on display at the HQ of the recently created space technology company Skyora.

On its arrival in Scotland a company spokesperson said the rocket could be: "The most important artefact linked to the UK's space history. While our engineers have been working on our own launches our ambassadors have been arranging all of this in the background." Britain's first astronaut, Helen Sharman, who was the first woman to visit Russia's Mir space station welcomed the return of a *Black Arrow*: "Looking at the *Black Arrow*, we can see how much science and engineering were needed to create it. I hope it will inspire people to find out more." Scotland's burgeoning space industry was also welcomed by Tim Peake, an astronaut who has spent time aboard the International Space Station and is supporting Skyrora's ambitions to become the UK's premier company for commercial rocket launches by joining the organisation's advisory board. Peake who hopes to return to space is well qualified for the task. He has seventeen years of experience in the military and aeronautical industry. In his six months stay on the ISS he managed experiments for hundreds of researchers back on earth.

In the summer of 2020 Skyrora's Volodymyr Levykin announced the launch of a four-metre rocket from a site in Iceland. The firm had previously successfully launched its "Skylark" *L* rocket from its site near Alness in the Highlands. This was to test systems to be used in the larger *Skyrora XL* intended to be launched from a UK spaceport in 2023. The Icelandic test rocket reached a height of seventeen miles above the earth. Mr Levykin told the *London Times*: "It is critical that we can complete the programme so that we can scale up and learn from any mistakes before launching our larger launch vehicles. The Icelandic launch allowed us to test our avionics and communications on a smaller and more cost-effective vehicle." He added that he was optimistic for the future of Britain's homegrown space industry. "We see this as being the first significant step towards reaching space from our own soil." Plans are progressing to create Britain's first vertical launch spaceport in Sutherland. Up to twelve launches of small commercial satellites that could be used for earth observation are planned. Another group in the mini-satellites business is AAC Clyde Space with an HQ in Glasgow and helping to collect data from space that "will tackle global challernges and improve life on earth".

Scotland's space industry has been growing swiftly. Already it is said that Glasgow helps manufacture more satellites than any city outside the USA. So far the emphasis has been on small research satellites, but hopefully the next stage will be launches both horizonal (from aircraft) and vertical in the style of Cape Canaveral, though on a smaller scale. And with the hardware reusable. As some of Elon Musk's experiments have already shown there is a growing market for swarms of micro satellites delivering data services.

Musk's ambitions, however, go far beyond the micro. Already Space X has taken a couple of astronauts to the ISS. And there is speculation that he could collaborate with NASA on a Mars mission. The breadth of the globalisation of satellite launching is demonstrated by the fact that Musk is involved in sending a top-secret satellite into orbit on behalf of the South Korean government. The military implications of this are obvious. Elon Musk has a fascinating range of interests, from electric cars to space exploration for its own sake and to aid the US military by placing GPS navigation systems in their desired orbit.

In Scotland getting into the launch business is far from as controversial as Musk. Data gathered will help fight climate change and improve communications on a worldwide scale. The ambition is big – David Oxley, of Highland and Islands Enterprise, one of the backers of the Sutherland Space Hub proposals, thinks Scotland has a lot in its favour in this new space race. He considers the natural advantages include the geographical suitability for access to orbits and flight paths and relative isolation from large centres of population. The success of the current programmes in Sutherland and other areas will be a step towards realising the aspiration of the Scottish Government of a £4 billion space industry by 2030.

Prestwick, too, has foothold in this tartan space race. The development of space launch services at Prestwick is being led by the airport and its partner South Ayrshire Council. In summer 2022 they announced they had already secured an £80 million funding boost through the Ayrshire Growth Deal to enable it to undergo a highly ambitious Aerospace and Space Programme and hopefully become the leading horizontal launch spaceport in Europe.

By 2035 the spaceport is intended "to provide a range of services, including air launch of satellites up to a mass of 800 kilograms, microgravity flights and hypersonic flights services". The first commercial rocket launches are hoped to take place from autumn 2023.

Prestwick Aerospace, located across the road from the main runway, has a cluster of aerospace companies – including Spirit AeroSystems, GE Caledonian, Collins Aerospace and BAE Systems. All this could create more than 4,000 new jobs, it is claimed.

Machrihanish, another site also has ambitions in this direction; one of the longest runways in Europe and Prestwick is in an excellent position for the concept of "piggyback" launches.

Currently, Branson concentrates his activities on Spaceport America in New Mexico close to the old White Sands Missile Range, not too far from El Paso. It has purpose-built hangars and a futuristic looking terminal. It is also far from large centres of population which is not a help in building a commercial airline hub to sit alongside the spaceport. Scotland has potential spaceports on the doorstops of large cities, and Branson's shiny new base has already been used for literally hundreds of commercial satellite launches and some impressive Virgin Galactic test jaunts into space. Despite one accident which killed the co-pilot, the craft had safely been taken to launch height by the mother ship, a converted *McDonnel Douglas* airliner, but a combination of pilot error and mechanical failure lost it. The spectacular failure and death in the desert was a setback, but not one that did anything to damage the concept of piggyback launches, or stop the man sometimes called "the bearded wonder" from taking a short trip in near space in one of his own craft.

From Percy Pilcher's hang gliders costing a few pounds for wood and cotton, and using the needlework skills of his own family, to enterprises costing and making millions ... "That is one small step for a Scotsman (or woman), one giant leap for Scotskind" as that honorary Borders Scot, Neil Armstrong might, or might not, have said. The dream so aptly labelled by Dugald Cameron as "From Pilcher to the Planets" is still alive.

Selected Sources and Suggested Further Reading

Roof of the World – Man's first flight over Everest by James Douglas-Hamilton (Mainstream, 1983)

Buffalo Airways – Home of the Ice Pilots by Daniel Cattoni and Lori Kerr (Icarus, 2012)

Chastise – The Dambusters by Max Hastings (William-Collins, 2019)

Fields of Deception – Britain's Bombing Decoys of World War II by Colin Dobinson (Methuen Publishing, 2000)

First Flight by Geoffrey Wellum (Penguin, 2003)

Wings Over Everest, a 1934 Oscar documentary available on YouTube

A Third Summer in Kintyre by Angus Martin (The Grimsay Press, 2016)

Diamond Flight – The story of British Midland by Bill Gunston (Henry Melland, 1988)

From Pilcher to the Planets by Dugald Cameron, Roderick Galbraith, Douglas Thomson (University of Glasgow, 2003)

The Airline Builders (Time-Life Books, 1981)

Loganair – A Scottish Survivor by Scott Grier (Kea Publishing, 2012)

Air Road to the Isles by Captain E Fresson (David Rendel Ltd, 1967)

Spitfire by John Nicol (Simon & Schuster, 2018)

The Sirens of Mars by Sarah Stewart Johnson (Allen Lane, 2020)

The Blackburn – Dumbarton's Aircraft Factory by Alan M Sherry (Stenlake Publishing, 1996)

Nine Lives by Al Deere (Amazon, 1999)

It's a Funny Life by Jimmy Logan (Black and White Publishing, 1998)

It Doesn't Matter Where You Sit by Fred McClement (Cassell, 1970)

Battle of Britain – the pilots and planes that made history by Simon Pearson and Ed Gorman (Hodder and Stoughton, 2020)

Fate is the Hunter by Ernest K Gann (Simon & Schuster, 1961)

A Boxing Dynasty by Tommy Gilmour (Black and White Publishing, 2007)

The Flying Scots by Jack Webster (The Glasgow Royal Concert Hall, 1994)

Luftwaffe Over Scotland: A History of German Air Attacks on Scotland, 1939–45 by Les Taylor (Whittles Publishing, 2010)

Deadly Peninsula – Military aircraft accidents on and around the Kintyre Peninsula by David W. Earl & Peter Dobson (Hanover Publications, 2018)

A Reluctant Icon: Letters to Neil Armstrong by James R Hansen (Perdue University Press, 2020)

The Flying Boat That Fell to Earth – A Lost World of Air Travel and Africa by Graham Coster (Safe Haven Books, 2019)

The Paisley Rocketeers by Donald Malcolm (Stenlake Publishing, 1997)

The Herald archives
The Scotsman archives
Daily Record Archives.
Dunoon Observer
Argyllshire Standard
The Press and Journal
The Times
The Scots Magazine
The Museum of Flight, East Fortune

Acknowledgements

Andrew Gordon, Sam Gordon, Nelson Gray, Dugald Cameron, Ronald Ross, Freddie Gillies, Grant Jeffrey, Peter Battison, Ron Atkin, Hugh McDiarmid, Frank Gallipeau, Stuart Jeffrey, Sian Jones, Rachel Morrell, Leslie McLeod, David Frost, Ray Bulloch, Tommy Gilmour, Marie Jeffrey, Jack Russell, Norrie Colquhoun, Ian McAdam, Scott Grier, Jimmy Logan, Harry Reid, Jimmy Turner, and the friendly staff at Glasgow's Mitchell Library, the Museum of Flight, East Fortune and at the Scottish National Museum, Edinburgh. Also, the shared memories of a flock of plane-spotting "anoraks" who enjoyed spending time on the long-forgotten viewing terraces of airports in the days before international terrorism.

Index

About the Author

Robert Jeffrey is a long-serving Glasgow journalist and the former managing editor of the Herald group of newspapers. His many best-sellers include:

Giants of the Clyde
Scotland's Cruel Sea
Peterhead – The Inside Story of Scotland's Toughest Prison
Gentle Johnny Ramensky
The Barlinnie Story
A Boxing Dynasty – The Tommy Gilmour Story
(with Tommy Gilmour)
Real Hard Cases: True Crime from the Streets
(with Les Brown)
Glasgow's Godfather
Gangs of Glasgow
Glasgow Crimefighter – The Les Brown Story
(with Les Brown)
Blood on the Streets – The A-Z of Glasgow Crime
The Wee Book of the Clyde
The Wee Book of Glasgow
Crimes Past – Glasgow's Crimes of the Century

Co-authored with Ian Watson:

Clydeside People and Places
The Herald Book of the Clyde
Doon the Watter
Scotland's Sporting Heroes
Images of Glasgow